Virginia Colonial Abstracts—Series 2, Vol. 6
Records of Prince George County, Virginia
1666–1719

Abstracted and Compiled by:
  The Rev. Lindsay O. Duvall

Southern Historical Press
Greenville, South Carolina

Copyright 1978
By: The Rev. Silas Emmett Lucas, Jr.

All rights reserved. No part of this publication may be reproduced, stored in a retrieval system, transmitted in any form, posted on to the web in any form or by any means without the prior written permission of the publisher.

Please direct all correspondence and orders to:

www.southernhistoricalpress.com
or
**SOUTHERN HISTORICAL PRESS, Inc.
PO BOX 1267
375 West Broad Street
Greenville, SC 29601
southernhistoricalpress@gmail.com**

ISBN #0-89308-067-5

Printed in the United States of America

Introduction

Most genealogists and students of Virginia history are familiar with the multi-volume work on early Virginia counties by the late Beverley Fleet. The Rev. Lindsay O. Duvall a former Rector of several Virginia Episcopal Churches was a friend and close associate of Mr. Fleet.

As best as your publisher has been able to find out, during the 1950's Mr. Duvall continued where Mr. Fleet left off with his Virginia Colonial Abstracts in what will be referred to as Series Two of these Colonial Abstracts; compiling five volumes himself and editing a sixth, being The Virginia Company of London which had been compiled by Mr. Fleet.

Few genealogists are familiar with Mr. Duvall's volumes because he did a very limited edition of each of the six titles; selling some and giving away others. Few Libraries have a complete set of Mr. Duvall's six titles. The Virginia State Library in Richmond has a complete set of Mr. Duvall's volumes which they have made available to the Publisher to reprint.

Because of the poor quality of mimeographing and paper used by Mr. Duvall in these volumes, it has been a very difficult and tedious task to try and re-type his material for this new edition of his work. There are many errors to be found which have not been corrected in this edition because we have transcribed exactly as Mr. Duvall printed in his originals. In some instances there will be errors on the publishers part of this new series because we were unable to read exactly what had been printed due to the poor quality of paper and mimeographing, as well as the fading and tearing of the paper in the originals. Should any question or confusion arise in studying this edition, the reader is advised to consult Mr. Duvall's originals in the Virginia State Library in Richmond. Hopefully these volumes will fill in many gaps in early Virginia genealogy and history.

Charles City County Land Patents, Books 6-9

Book 6

p. 39. Robert Burgesse, 343 Acres, 105 po. Bounded at a marked oaks 4 ways, being a corner tree of Gilbert Platt, and running unto ye woods upon a line of Robert Colemans S.E. by S. 45 po., then S.E. & by E. 32 po. upon the land of Robt. Coleman Jr., then S.W. & by S. 320 po., then N.W. by W. 131 po., to the head line of Gilbert Platt, along this line E.N.E., then N.N.W. 356 po. to the beginning. The sd. land is on the S. side of Appomattox River, and is due for the Trans. of 7 psons., 12 Nov. 1666. (7 named.)
George Armestrong   Robert Terrill   Anth: Gardners   An Marble
Mathew Jones   Eliz: Colery   Wm. Sattervaile

p. 62. Lt. Col. John Epes, 2550 Acres, 32 R., 16 po., S. side of Ja: River, commonly known by the name of Charles City. Bounded: ber. at the mouth of Grabelly Cr. at the Riv. --- 500 po. by ye Cytte landing, thence W. & S. to Caresons Cr. -- to a tree, now in possession of John Howell, to Gowens Corner --- to the Cattle Br. --- to Mr. Whittingtons Corner tree --- to Cattle Br. --- to Ban- (mutilated) Cr. --- to ye Branch at Colem(ans) feild--- to the mouth of Baylyes Cr. --- to be beginning. The Land is due: 1700 Acres hereof being granted to Capt. ffra. Epes by Patt. 29 May 1638 & due ye sd. John as Sonn & heire of his father ye sd. ffran. & 280 Acres, another part hereof, granted to Col. ffran. Epes by Patt. 14 Ma (mutilated) 1663, & due to Lt. Col. Jno. Epes as son, etc.

p. 63

and 572 Acres ye residue by Trans. of 11 psons., 30 Sept. 1674 (date as is).
Robert Bennett   Peter Seaman   Rich'd. Wright
Elm. ffrith   Sarah Smith   Rich'd. Crawshaw
Hump.: fferick   Sarah Richer   John Maude
Jno. Lewis   Wm. Brush

p. 85. William Wilkins, 472 Acres, 3 R., 1 po., at the head of fflewerdee Cr. en the E. side of the Southern run joyning to Wm. Harris. Bounded: on Southern run, S.S.E. -- The sd. land being due by Trans.: of 10, 13 March 1665.

Teage Okey   Tho: Grice   Zach: Ellmer
Rise Joanes   Edward Alloster   Richard Smith
Anne Joanes   Gerard Greene
ffrancis Chandler   ffrancis Outeley

p. 85. William Wilkins, 300 Acres, 3 R., 31 po., S. side of Ja: Riv., head of fflowerdee hundred Cr. Bounded: --- at an oak --- to a path named Blands path --- to the beginning. 200 Acres of this Land was purchased of Richard Pace, as by Chas. City Co. Records, & 100 Acres, & 8 Acres, 3 R., 31 po. are due by Trans. of 3, 13 April 1666.
Saml. Warren   James Bird   Thomas Davis

p. 86. Wm. Harrison, Jr., 368 Acres, 3 R., 37 po., S. side of Ja: Riv. Bounded: --- to a white oake in a line of Capt. David Peoples --- to the corner of Robt. Joanes --- to Pyny Sw. --- to ye old Town Bridge --- to a bottom which runneth out of the Reddy bottom --- to a line of Mr. Rich'd. Tye --- to the beginning. The sd. Land is due by the Trans. of 7 pers. (not named), 5 April 1667.

p. 90. The Parish of Martin Brandon, 200 Acres for a Gleebe belonging to their Church, lying betwixt Capt. Johnsons land and the Marchants, beginning at a marked oak standing on the banke at the Watering place --- upon the River --- to beginning, 5 December 1667.

p. 134. John Maies, Sonne of Wm: Maies dec'd., 293 Acres, 2 R., 33 po., on the S. side of Appomattock River, 125 Acres, part thereof, being part of a former Patent of 250 Acres granted to Ed. Townstall & by him sold to Wm. Maies, father to the sd. Jno. Maies, adj. to sd. Maies' land next to the River. Bounded --- by a great Sw., being at the head of the sd. Maies Island (text: Inland?) Patent --- along Samll. Woodwards side line -- to the lower end of the Great Sw. --- to the beginning. 168 Acres, part thereof, is due for the Trans. of 4 psons., 29 April 1668.
Jno. Bird   Sarzel berry   Jeremy Right   Wm. Belnett

(p. 134, from the No County Index. Henry Leadbeater, 224 Acres, S. side of Appamattock Riv. Bounded: 99 Acres, 3 R. --- at a corner tree of Robt. Colemans at the head of his land where he now lives --- to the beginning. 125 Acres thereof, being a part of a former Patent of 250 Acres Granted to Ed: Tunstall & by him sold to the sd. Leadbeater's father. 99 Acres, part thereof, being due for the Trans. of 2 psons., 29 April 1668.
Margery Lucas   Mary House.)

p. 142. Mr. Elias Osborne, 200 Acres, S. E. side of Wards Cr. Bounded: by the side of the Cr. at the mouth of Hanocks bottom --- at Mr. Bird's line --- to the beginning. The land is due by the Trans. of 4 psons., 1 June 1668.
John Osborne, Wm. Osborne, Elias Osborne, Joseph Osborne.

p. 182. Wm. Pebles, 862 Acres, 2 R., S. side of Ja: Riv. Bounded: 473 Acres 3 R., 24 po., part thereof, beginning on a line formerly surveyed for Tho: Newhouse --- to ye Birchen Sw. --- to the beginning. 388 Acres, 2 H., 16 po., the residue, --- at the head of a Bottome nigh ye old Towne Land --- to ye Westward of Thos. Newhouse his corner to the beginning. There is due 473 Acres, 3 R., 24 po., by Patent 30 July 1670; the remainder being 388 Acres, 2 R., 16 p., by Trans. of 7 psons., 3 Nov. 1673.
Hen: Madebey   Jno: Trahoane   Mary Gibbons
Rob:r Cooke   Eliz: Jettly   The: And:rson
Mary Bennett

p. 189. Robert Coleman, Sr., 283 Acres, 14 po., S. side of Appamattox Riv. 207 Acres thereof formerly granted to Mr. Walter Chiles and by him sold & assigned to sd. Robt. Coleman Sr. 2 Acres at the head thereof was granted to Henry Leadbeater and by him sold & assigned to the sd. Coleman, & the residue thereof being lately taken up and bounded: --- at the river being a corner tree between Henry Leadbeater & the sd.

Coleman --- to Poiney Sw. --- to the beginning. The sd. land
is due for the Trans. of 2, 29:7ber:1668.
Tho: Pampin   Wm. Jenkins

    p. 203. Capt. ffrancis Epps, 1980 Acres, S. side of Ja:
Riv. on the S. side of Appamattox Riv. 280 Acres, S. on Capt.
Batts --- on the head of Walter Brookes (,) Nich. Tatum &
Jno. Bakers Land. 700 Acres, being formerly granted to the
sd. ffrancis Epps by Patent, 23 an. 1653 & renewed in the name
of his by Patent 17 March 1663 & 1700 Acres, the residue,
formerly granted to the sd. Capt. Epps, 29 May 1638 & bounded:
--- upon Baylys Cr. --- upon Casons Cr., up Appomattock Riv.
& N. on the Main Riv., 4 Oct. 1668.

    p. 227. Mr. Tho: Newhouse, 1050 Acres, S. side of Ja:
Riv. Bounded: --- nyth (nigh) Mr. Sparrow his land --- to
Burchen Sw. --- to the beginning. The land was due by Trans.
of 21 psons.: 15 July 1669.

Edward Ellis	Ellener ffowke	Danl. Lawmun
Roger Risese	Tho. Mallory	Ann Danby
Hugh Barrow	Jno. Bardoe	Jno. Cromwell
Judith Avery	Ja: Cabbock	Jno. Yapp
ffra: Poysen	Lawr: Ellis Jun:r.	David a Scotchman
Wm. Hind	Jno. Ball	Tho. ffitchett
John Ward	James Okeldry	(Note: only 20 are given.)

    p. 241. Jno. Howell, a Dev'd. called Bakers, 203 Acres,
32 po., nigh the mouth of Appomottox Riv. Bounded: at a gut
parting Nath. Tatum & the sd. Howell --- to the cleare feild
--- to Cawsons Cr. --- to the beginning. This land was formerly granted to the sd. Howell for a greater grant of acres,
but upon resurvey it is found but the quantity above. 18
Aug. 1669.

    p. 246. Wm. Harrison (which side is not stated, but
possibly here), 300 Acres, being part of a Patent granted to
Jno. ffreeme, escheated, Inq., Mr. Hen: Randolph, Deply
Esch'r. for the sd. Co. (of Chas. City) & Jury 18 June 1668,
being granted to Tho. Calloway & now granted to the sd. Wm.
Harrison, 24 July 1669.

    p. 247 (it possibly beongs here, the side not being
named), Mr. Anthony Wyatt, 398 Acres, granted to George Potter
dec'd., lately escheated, Inq. before Mr. Hen. Randolph,
Dep'y. Esch'r. for the Co. (Chas. City), Jury 16 June 1668,
granted now to Anthony Wyatt, 24 July 1669.

    p. 247 (possibly belongs here, the side not being named.)
Mr. Morris Rose, 300 Acres, formerly granted to Tho. Cole,
escheated, Inq. before Mr. Hen. Randolph, Dep'y. Esch'r. for
the Co. (Chas. City), Jury 16 June 1668, now granted to Morris
Rose, 24 April 1669.

    p. 248 (possibly belongs here, the side not named), John
West, 100 Acres, granted to John Pratt dec'd. & lately escheated, Inq. before Mr. Hen. Randolph, Dep'y Esch'r. for the Co.
(Chas. City), 22 June 1668, now granted to John West, 24 July
1669.

    p. 248 (possibly belongs here, the side not named), Mr.
James Wallace, 990 Acres, formerly granted to Tho. Wheeler,

dec'd., lately escheated, Inq. before Hen: Randolph, Dep'y Esch'r. for the Co. (Chas. City), Jury 18 June 1668, now granted to James Wallace, 24 July 1669.

p. 273. Mr. Tho. Busby, 194 Acres. Bounded: --- a poplar standing by the rim of the Westerne Br. of Upp(er) Chipokes Cr. --- the Southern Br. --- to the beginning. 95 Acres, part thereof, was formerly granted to Jno. Rawlins & Mich. Mittaine by Patent 10 May 1667 & by them sold & assigned to the sd. Busby. 90 Acres, the residue, was due by the Trans of 2, 16 April 1669 (the acreage is short & possibly this should read 99 Acres.)
Robert Busby   Wm. Emons.

p. 285. Mr. Wm. Batt, 700 Acres, in the branches of Bylies Cr. Bounded: --- by the James Warrendine land called High Peake & now in the occupation of Mr. Wm. Ditty & Robt. Langman --- to the beginning. The land was formerly granted to Robt. West, Patent 2 (? - written ever and thus difficult to read) Aug. 1652 & new renewed to ye sd. Wm. Batt, as by a surrender in Chas. City Court 3 Aug. 1653, the land being formerly due to ye sd. Robt. West by Trans of 14 (not named here), 22 April 1670.

p. 286. James Thweate, 600 Acres, S. side of Appamatox Riv. Bounded:--- on Baylys Cr. --- to Robt. Coleman Jr. his land --- to the beginning. The sd. land was due by Trans. of 12 psons. 20 April 1670.
Willm. Williams   Jno. Williams   Jno. Hobson
Sarah Leage   Eliz. Williams   Mary Hobson
Geo: Davis   James Thweat   Wm. Neting
Rachell Williams   Jno. Lawrence   Edward Price

p. 289. William Pebles, 473 Acres, S. side of Ja: Riv. Bounded: on a line formerly surveyed for Tho: Newhouse --- to the Birchen Sw. --- to the beginning. The sd. land was due for the Trans. of 10, 30 July 1670.
James Durrant   James Dent   John Grimshaw
John Minter   Christo: Brown   Giles Wright
ffra. Hawgood   Oathawin Jenkin   Will. Langland
Tho. Tomlinson

p. 292. Wm. Heath, 378 Acres, Surry Co. & Chas. City Co. Bounded: --- on the S. side of Appawhipoats (the letters ts are clouded by a letter written over them) Cr. --- a white oak upon The Shepherds land --- on the N. side of a Great Sw. --- to the beginning. The sd. land was due: 250 Acres purchased of Will. Lee. & 50 Acres purchased of Will. Shorts & the residue being 78 Acres, which is due by the Trans. of 2 psons., 23 Oct. 1669.
Himself & Sarah Killotty.

p. 317. William Peble, 473 Acres, 3 R., 24 po., S. side of Ja. Riv. Bounded: on a line --- to Birchen Sw. --- to the beginning. The sd. land was due by trans. of 10 psons., 30 July 1670.
James Durrant   James Dent   Jno. Grimshaw
Jno. Minter   Xopher Browne   Giles Wright
ffra. Hawgood   Ratherme Jenkin   Wm. Langland
Tho. Tomlyn (Note: the above and this are examples of differ-
                    ing details.)

p. 326. Thomas Reynolds, 50 Acres. Bounded: --- to a small white oake --- to the beginning. The sd. 50 Acres in Martin Brandon Parish, were given him by Mark Avery by Deed of Guift, 8 April 1660, Ack. in Chas. City o. Court 3 Oct. 1660 by sd. M. A. & Rec. 20 Oct. 1660. Patent: 14 Oct. 1670.

p. 327. Mr. Michael Hill, 220 Acres, 16 po., on the S. side of Appomattock Riv. Bounded: --- at a corner tree of Walter Brooke his land to Jno. Sturdevants land --- to the beginning. The sd. land was due by Trans. of 5 psons., 15 Oct. 1670.

Jno. Armstrong	Mary Greene	Derry Grymes
Wm. Inke	Robt. Dyamond	

p. 404. Edward Greenwood, 281 Acres, on the N. side of Upper Chipoaks Cr. against Swan Bay. Bounded from the Cr. --- to the beginning. The sd. land was due by the Trans. of 5 psons. (not names), (originally dated) 19 Nov. 1651; this patent is dated 25 April 1672.

p. 406. Ralph Rachell, 200 Acres, on the S. E. side of Wards Cr. Bounded: on the Creeks side at the mouth of Hannocks bottom --- along the sd. bottom & Mr. Birds line --- at the Mussell shell banck --- to the beginning. The Land was formerly granted to Elias Osborne by Patent 1 June 1668 & by the sd., Osborne assigned to sd. Rachell 28 Jan. 1670. This: 28 Jan. 1670.

p. 446. Edward Birchett, 351 Acres, 32 po., on the S. side of Appomattock Riv. Bounded: at a corner of Mr. Henry Batts land, next to James Thweate --- to the beginning. The sd. land was due by the Trans. of 7 psons., 15 March 1672/3.

Alis Mobell	Elinor Woodcock	Mary Davis
Ellinur Bottomly	Catherine Crosse	George Bankse
George Mercer		

p. 447. James Thweate, 550 Acres, on the S. side of Appomatock Riv. Bounded: at Robt. Colemans line where James Thweate his line joynes --- to the Blackwater --- to the great Meddow --- to the beginning. The sd. land was due by Trans. of 13 psons. (The text says 650, the margin says 550 Acres, and there are 13 to account for 650 Acres,) 15 March 1672/3.

Hercules fflood	Roger Jones	Winifred Prior
Edward Young	James Thweate	Peter Jones
An: ffaulner	Margaret Matherse	James ffarler
Tho: Hopp	Mary Bonner	John Throer
	Rebecca: Robinson	

p. 480. Hugh Lee, 1374 Acres, 2 R., on th S. side of Appomatock Riv. Bounded: at a corner formerly marked for the sd. Lee --- to the Balckwater ---. The sd. Land was due by the Trans. of 27 psons., 28 Oct. 1673.

Richard Cutson	Martha Hiatt	Tho: Williams
Andrew Hudenford	Simon Harwood	Hugh Lee 7 times
Elizabeth Hughes	John West	Elizabeth Downing
ffrancis Higgs	Katherine ffry	Elizabeth Downing
Jiremiah Hutt	Hugh Lee	Will. Downing his son & daughter
John Burrage	Ann Lee	
Margaret Edwards	Johan Davis	

p. 480. Hen: Batts & Mr. Jno: Sturdivant, 3528 Acres, on the S. side of Appomatock Riv. Bounded: on the second Br. of Blackwater --- to the beginning. The sd. land was due by the Trans. of 71 psons., 28 Oct. 1673. (The headrights are listed on the next page.)

Tho: Williams	Wm. Hurdings	Wm: Browne
John James	David Anderson	James Atkins
Rich'd. Dearelove	Patrick Jorden	Ja: Alder
Wm. Dobson	Jno. Burgained	Rich: Adler
Teage	Morice George	Rich: Brise
Jno. Barlow	Ja. Marchant	Ed: Ladd
Jno. Tovey	Wm. Crowder	Robt: Haley
Joseph Tovey	Mary Hust	Hen: Prefird
Rase: Brechinhead	Eliz. Dyer	Ja: Bradshaw
Phill. Bowley	Moll Browne	Wm: Barker
Chris: Hinton	Eliz: Arnold	Godfrey Wynn
Han: Barlow	Wm: Brannard	Jno: Hughes
Ja: Cappoke	Jno: Storidge	Gabriell Jones
Kath: Huson	Phill. Gledger	Sus: Edwards
John Lee	Tho: Holmes	Prissilla Lane
Edw'd. Shomake	John Thompson	Mich Pallman
Susanah Mallory	Walter Gay	Chris: Pecke
Edw'd. Hanakin	Robt: Jurvor(?)	Tho: Wallow
Tho. Mallory twice	Jeffrey Nash	Wm: Howard
Griffeth Evens	Theod: Moore	Cha: Mason
Mungo a negro	Dan: Care	Wm: Brett
Ja: Creneds (?) 4 times	Hugh Griffen	Phill. Anderson
	ffra: Reynolds	Rebecca Salter

p. 481. Will Bobbett, 95 Acres, 3 R., 24 Po., on the S. side of Appomatock Riv. Bounded: --- nigh Mr. Whittington his line --- along Maj. Epes his line --- by Cattale Br. --- to the beginning. The sd. land was due by Trans. of 2, 27 Oct. 1673. John Lead & Richard Tonstall.

p. 481. John Maies, 89 Acres, 23 po., on the S. side of Appomatock Riv. Bounded: Easterly end of the Long Slash nigh Samuell Woodward his head line --- to John Maies his line --- along the Great Sw. --- to the beginning. The sd. land was due by the Trans. of 2 psons., 27 Oct. 1673.
Philemon Childers   Tho: Crompton

p. 484. ffrancis Whittington, 1200 Acres, on the S. side of Appomattock Riv. Bounded: at the head of Baylyes Cr. --- to the beginning. 900 Acres of the sd. land being formerly granted to Tho: and Henry Batts & by them sold to the sd. Whittington, and 300 Acres was the residue, which was due by the Trans. of 6 psons., 30 Oct. 1673.
Barth. Batts   Robt. Unebill (?)   Mary Mahames
Jno. Cumber   Jno. Collins   Elizab. Wood

p. 486. Edward Birchett, 551 Acres, 320 po., on the S. side of Appomatock Riv. Bounded: 351 Acres, 32 po., part thereof, at a corner of Hen: Batt his land next James Thweate. The residue, 200 Acres, is bounded: on the westerly Runn of Bailies Cr. --- to the old line parting James Thweate & this survey --- nigh the Blackwater --- to the beginning. 351 acres, 320 po. was due sd. Birchett by Patent 15 March 1672 & the residue of 200 Acres was part of the Spring Garden Patent bought of Hen: Batts, as by the Records of Bristoll Court may appear, 31 Oct. 1673.

p. 488. Rich. Taylor, 1000 Acres, on the S. side of Ja:
Riv. on the Blackwater behind Marchants hope. Bounded: at a
Sw. --- to bhe beginning. The land was given by the Last Will
of Rich'd. Taylor his father, dated 15 July 1672. This Patent
is 3 Nov. 1673. The names (all) under the patent.

Tho: Mayson	Eliz. Scarbroob	Aylse Asley (?)
Pollidor Rich'd.	Hen: Roberts	Anne Towsing
Rich'd. Putman	Tho. Anderson	Rich'd. Stafford
Jo: Davis	Oliver Davenport	Tho. Jones
Jno. Adams	Ellen ffairclots	Eliz. Herd
	Susan ffairbrother	Wm. Hewgille

p. 488. Robt. Lucy, 1000 Acres, on the S. side of the Ja:
Riv. on the Blackwater in a certain place called Saw tree.
Bounded: adj. to the land of Rich'd. Taylor --- between the
land of the sd. Rich'd. Taylor & Robt. Lewry. The sd. land
was due by the Trans. of 20 psons., 3 Nov. 1673

Neph. (?) Ryland	Mary Doer	Wm. Walker
Jno. Butler	Susan Marsh	John Shelly
Phill. Gorman	Rich'd. Combe	Prisila Chena
Mary Sawer	Riddy Ashday	Rich'd. Taylor
Roger Poynton	Rob: Wyatt	Ann Godfry
Eliz. Strickland	John Dorrell	Rich'd. Taylor
Tho: Cribis (?)	Roger Miller	

p. 509. James Hall, 302 Acres, 3 R., 12 po., on the S.
side of Appamattock Riv. Bounded: at the mouth of a Cr.
parting the Land of Mr. Wm. ffarrar & Xopher Woodward --- to
a slash --- to the beginning. The sd. land was due by the
Trans. of 6 psons., 8 April 1674.

Ja: Washbrooke	Ja: Hall	Tho. Hind
Robt. Ward	Cha: Stuard	Samll. Moyson

p. 509. Wm. W(illia)ms, 331 Acs., on the S. side of
Appamattocks Riv. Bounded: beginning where Samll. Woodward
his line runneth, 100 po. from the Cr. parting Mr. ffarrar &
ye sd. Woodward --- to the beginning. Of this land, 291 Acres
were first sold by Samll. Woodward to Mr. Antho: Wyatt as by
assignment, 8:8ber:1650 & from the sd. Wyatt to Robt. Burges,
23 Jan. 1655 & from the sd. Burges to Wm. Wms., 20:bris:
1660, as p. Bristow Cort appear, & by the Trans. of 1 pson.,
8 April 1674. Rich'd Wright.

p. 510. Hercules fflood, 470 Acres, 1 R., on the S. side
of Appamattock Riv. Bounded: beginning at Wm. James (as is)
--- a Br. of the Blackwater --- to the beginning. The sd. land
was due by the Trans. of 9 psons., 8 April 1674.

Sara Hill Sr.	Robt. Rich'son	Ann Thomas
Sara Hill Jr.	Jno. Habson	Wm. Hobbing
Mihill Hill Jr.	Jno. Addams	Tho. Gregerins

p. 510. Wm. Jones (this name may be Jomes), 470 Acres,
1 R., on the S. side of the Appamattock Riv. Bounded: at a
corner formerly surveyed for hercules fflood --- to the Blackwater --- to the beginning. The sd. land was due for the
Trans. of 9 psons., 8 April 1674.

Tho. Killdolls	Ann Peterson	Mihill Jackson
Wm. Butler	David Goodale	Ann Moone
Rich'd. Watson	David Good	Wm. Jones

p. 510. Hugh Lee, 2000 Acres, on the S. side of Appamattock Riv. Bounded: on the N. side of the third Br. of the Blackwater --- to the beginning. The sd. land was due for the Trans. of 40 psons., 8 April 1674.

Rich'd. Spakes	Tho: Clark	Cha: Bartlett
Hen: Neale	Jno. Browne	Wm. Taylor
Jno. Crew	Tohnasin (?) fforine (?)	Jno: ffloyd
Andr: Crew	Phill. Pledge	Tho: Lipwell
Rich: Dennis	Mary Browne	Sara King
Wm. Marsh	Jno. Cox	Rebecca Lome
Massis Joyce	Rich'd. Warren	Sara Swellame
Hen: Allaman	Tho: Michell	Jacobus Jonson
Jno. Browne	Jno. Trenmett (?)	Robt. Hyde
Wm. Bernard	Barbara Petingall	Martha Gibbs
Eliz. Cooper	Jno. Burges	Robt. Hicks
Tho. Woods	Tho. Ovy	Jno. Allen
Thos: Tance	Addam Bradshaw	Tho. Alsen

p. 529. Edward Richards, 1528 Acres, on the S. side of the Ja: Riv. Bounded: below the Ponds nigh the head of Neards Cr. --- to the Boggy Br. nigh a small Indian ffeild --- to the Southern Run --- to the beginning. Of the sd. Land, 750 Acres was formerly gr'te(d), to Jno. Nescropa by Patent 30 Aug. 1650 & by him sold to John Graves (or Granes) & Tho. Morgan, 29 July 1653 & the sd. Morgan sold the sd. Edw'd. Richards (it), 10 Jan. 1654. The residue is 775 Acres, and is due by the Trans. of 16 psons., 26 Sept. 1674.

Wm. Jones	Rich'd. Right	Mary Dransell
Tho: Alford	Tho: Trainer	John Martin
Rich'd. Nesdin	Hugh Morganhuragon	Tho: Cooper
Wm. Browne	Christopher Gavsy	Inghambed Anderson
Ann Browne	fran: Bird	
Tho: Browne	Hannah Townesend	

p. 553. James Wallace, 738 Acres, on the S. side of Ja: Riv. Bounded: on the Blackwater at the E. end of Robt. Lucy his land --- over the Cattaile Br. --- to the Sw. --- to the beginning. The sd. land was due by the Trans. of 15 psons., 26 Feb. 1674/5.

Tho. Taylor	Jno: Nicholas	Elin:r Norton
Jno. Wood	Phill. Yeates	Robt: Lewes
Ben: Tood	Mary Kennon	Martin Graine
And: Teck	Edd. Annitt	Demmat Donnell
Rich: Cake	Jno: Langford	Sarah Hind

p. 613. Robert Netherland, 490 Acres, on the N. side of fflower de hundred Cr. Bounded: N. on land formerly purchased by Mr. Pace --- upon the woods. The sd. land was formerly granted to Tho: Drew, Gent., dec'd., by Patent 4 June 1657 & not seated according to the promise of the same, escheated & granted to the sd. Robt. Netherland by order of the General Court, 7 March last & is due by the Trans. of 10 psons., 15 June 1676. Under the Patent:

Jno. Wilson	Robt. Prester	Negro Thoms
Tho. Hilliard	Tho: Arch	

Book 7

(p. 24, No County Index. Saml. Woodward, 870 Acres, upon Appamatuck Riv. Bounded: 600 Acres, formerly taken up & Patented by Chris. Woodward, 24 Aug. 1637, and is due to the sd. Sam. as heir to ye sd. Chris. & bounded: N. upon the River --- E. upon land belonging to Mr. Farran, Gent., upon ye Winding River & 270 Acres, the residue, & the land is due the sd. Sam. Woodward for the Trans. of 6 psons. & being in the Parish of Bristol on the S. side of Appamatuck Riv. & in ye county of Chas. City, between Samll. Woodward & the River & the land is called Baylys on ye head of ye lands of Mr. John Mayes on ye Southward & ye lands in possession of Ja: Hall --- to Mr. Hen: Newcombs corner tree --- near Hofford & near Hoffords Plantation & Hoffords Run to ye Kings Road, 20 April 1680. The Patent is incomplete - L.O.D.
3 Negroes Robt. Stanly   Wm. Cobutt   Ellen Roach.)

p. 29. Robt. Tucker, 172 Acres, an irregular tract of Land on the N. side of the Blackwater. Bounded: on the Blackwater --- to a corner of Wm. Jones his land --- to Jordans path --- to Edw'd. Bircherds corner --- to the Reedy Br. The sd. land is due by the Trans. of 4 psons., 20 April 1680.
Jno. Tucker 3 times & Sar: Isvill.

p. 30. Wm. Vaughan, 1225 Acres, 32 po., on the S. side of Appamatuck Rev. Bounded: 100 Acres thereof being part of 150 Acres, formerly purchased of Hugh Lee, lying on ye James side of Appamatuck Riv., adj. the land of Tho: Lowe; 100 Acres, part thereof, formerly purchased of Robt. Burges, lying on the S. side of Appamatuck Riv. & along the line of Hen: Chanus --- to the beginning: 720 Acres, part thereof, lying on the S. side of Appamatuck Riv. adj. Jno. Ewens & Wm. Johnson & Robert Coleman; to the heads of Burgis, Colson; Lear & part of Tho: Lows land; 720 Acres were formerly assigned to the sd. Vaugh an by Hugh Lee & Wm. Battow & Gill Pratt; 305 Acres, 32 po., the residue, lying on the S. side of Appamatuck Riv. --- down ye Blackwater, adj. Hugh Lee --- to the beginning, and is due by the Trans. of 7 psons.,
Jno: Peterson   Susan Holsworth   Rich'd. Spenlyn
Geo: Levett   Robt: Iybaulds   Elias Tegamy
Tho: Stroud

p. 45. Maj. Gener:ll Abraham Wood, 1304 Acres, Parish of Bristoll, on the S. side of the run of Appamattuck Riv. & to Westward of his former D'v'dt. & near the Indian Towne Cr. --- run of Appamattuck Riv. opposite to the lands of Mr. Thomas Batts. The sd. land was due by the trans. of 27 psons., 10 July 1680.
ffr. Conaway   Tho: Edwards   ffra. Child
Margtt. ffarrar   Wm. ffleming   Rebecca Sandy
Robt. Harrison   Mary fflood   Ann Grant
B. Prasock   Tho. Moore   Susan Leach
Ed. Savage   Edw'd. Brichett   Jno. Jacob
Tho: Benington   Hen: Manering   Renne Blake
Mary Green   Nich: Overber   Anth. Wishett
Jno. Bevins   Rich: Phillips   Sanders Brus
Nich. Brooke   Jno. Blacksho   Mart Trydon

p. 45. Henry Newcomb, 549 Acres, 4 R., 22 po., 387 Acres, 2 R. thereof on the S. side of Appamattuck--at the Citty Crooke S.W. along the line of Samuel Woodward

p. 46
to the Northern Br. of Balys Cr.; 216 Perches & 162 Acres & 22 po. therof on the S. side of Appamattuck Riv., in the Parish of Bristoll, adj. John Mayes---to Baylys Path---to the line of Mr. Robert Coleman---to the beginning. Of this land, 287 Acres, 2 R. was granted to the sd. Newcombe by Patent 15 Feb. 1663; the residue is due by trans. of 4 psons., 10 July 1680.
Tho. Wethrington, Dorothy Egdole, & John Gavill are all who are named.

p. 99. ffrancis Poy thres (margin: Poytheres) 609 Acres, 2 R., 9 po., an irregular tract on the Blackwater, on the S. side of Ja: Riv. Bounded on the S. side of the Blackwater---to the Nottaway Path---to the first Br.---to the second Br.---to the line of Capt. Robt. Lowry containing 50 Acres, thence up the Maine Sw.---to the beginning. The sd. land was due by the Trans. of 12 psons (not named). 28 Sept. 1681.

p. 101. Mr. John Smith, an irregular tract, 306 Acres, R., 38 po., on the S. side of the Blackwater at a place called Norrobhocke, in the Parish of Bristoll, bounded on a small gumm standing in the second Br. of the Blackwater, adj. Hugh Lee---crossing the house path Br.---to the beginning. The sd. land was due for the Trans. of 6 psons. (not named), 24 Sept. 1681.

p. 122. Joshua Meatcham, 292 Acres, on the N. side of the Blackwater Parish of Westover. Bounded: from a corner white oake of Mr. James Wallis, along Capt. Busbies line to the sd. Busbies Corner standing upon the Maine Sw. The sd. land was due for the trans. of 6 psons., 20 April 1682.
Wm. Gatersone   Tho: Horons   Katherine
Rich'd. Broneley   Jno. Edloo   Mary Ellis

p. 124. Wm. Edmonds & John William, 888 Acres 2 R., 16 po., on the S. side of the Ja: Riv., Parish of Jordans. Bounded: at a corner gumm of Maj. Poytries standing upon the Reddy Br.---to a Great Br. (also Ready Br.) to the Round Pond. The sd. land was due by Trans. of 20 psons., 20 April 1682.
Fra: Linsley   Nich: Whitmore   Sander Hempseed
Gilbert Hay   Priscilla Chenye   John Allett
Wm. Turpin   Susanna Bridge   Ellinor Madard
Wm. Brown   James Blamore   Mary Horbord
George Buree   Xopher Addison   Mary Phillips
Thomas Manning   Jean Booth   (All who are named)

p. 130. (possibly belongs here.) Maj. Francis Poytries, 750 Acres, which Thomas Morgan died seized of, escheated, Inq. before Henry Hartwell, Dep'y. Esch'r., Jury 3 August 1681, now granted to the sd. Poytries, 20 April 1682.

p. 138. John Wanpoole, 216 Acres. Bounded: the N. side of the Western Br. of upper Chipeakes Cr.---a corner tree of

Wm. Keaths land---to the beginning. The sd. land was formerly surveyed for Thomas Steevens & is due the sd. Wanpoole in right of his wife Sarah, the daughter of the sd. Steevens and by Trans of 5 psons., 20 April 1682.

An Wilcocks John Thomas Onelius Scriven
Mary Bankes Hannah Hemsteed

p. 150. Hen: Bates & James Thweat, 673 Acres, 2 R., 6 po., on the S. side of Ja. Riv., Parish of Jordanes, and bounded: upon the line of Mr. Jon. Wingame---to a corner white oake of Mr. William Edmonds---upon the line of Mr. Edward Adington---to the beginning. The sd. land was due by Trans. of 14 psons., 20 April 1682.

Law: Fleming   Eliz. Kendall   Id., Timothy, Allen, Jack,
Rich'd. Longwell   Barbara Young   Cophell & Tango,
Faith Springwell   Eusebius King   Negroes (Timoth is
Gee. Hatter   Robt. Evans   the spelling of above)

p. 164. Henry Armstrong, 198 Acres, 1 R., 16 po., on the N.W. side of Upper Chipoakes Cr., the Parish of Martin Brandon & on the S. side of Ja. Riv. Bounded: on the Cr. side--- along the line of Wm. Short, crossing the Cold Spring---to the line of Mr. Nich. Perry---crossing the Cold Spring slash--- to the beginning. The sd. land is due for the Trans. of 4 psons., 29 April 1682.

James Cann   Eliz. Shaplys
Rich Atkinson   Hen: White

p. 175. (possibly belongs here.) Elias Osborne, 50 Acres which Jane Osborne died seized of, escheated, Inq., before Henry Hartwell, Dep'y. Esch'r., Jury 3 Aug. 1681, now granted to the sd. Elias Osborne, 20 April 1682.

p. 192. Thomas Cunitton, 150 Acres, on the S. side of Ja. Riv., in Westover Parish. Bounded: on the S. side of Ja. Riv. & dry bottom run, thence along a line of James Mountford---down the Slash of dry bottom run---to the line of Mr. Warradine---to the head of Woolfe Slash---to a corner black oake nigh Kings road---to the beginning. The sd. land was due by Trans. of 3 psons., 22 Sept. 1682.

Saml1. Marshall   Robt: Bittern   Reginald Anderson

p. 199. Wm. Randolph & Robert Bolling, Gent., 623 Acres 14 po., in the Parish of Bristoll & on the S. side of Appamattox Riv. at a Sw. named Waughnick Sw. Bounded: at a corner trii of Hugh Lees---upon the great meadow---to the main sw.--- to the beginning. The sd. land was due by the Trans. of 13 psons., 20 Nov. 1682.

Jon: Witt   Lidid Sawyer   Tho: Jones
Tho: Gewer   Lyon: Britton   Job:
Rich: Brown   Joh: Harnold   Jane Borar
Tho: Lyborne   Peter Frout   Edw. Gower
Robt. Beazley

p. 216. Mr. Jno. Evans, 557 Acres 31 po., on the S. side of Hepouatuck Riv., in the Parish of Xristoll. Bounded: on the line of Maj. Gen. Wood---standing on the Southern run, crossing the main Ready Br.

crossing the Western Br.---to the beginning. The sd. land was due by Trans. of 12 psons., 22 Dec. 1682.

Tho: Stacy	Jon: Smith	Margt. Turner
Hen: West	Adam Miles	Eliz. Porter
Mary West	Matt: Wilson	Nicho: Porter
Robt. Woodby	Jon: Midleton	James Tanner

p. 237. Richard Williamson, 307 Acres, on the S. side of Ja. Riv., Parish of Wayonoake, at a place called the Otter Dams at a corner white oake of John Harris---to the Otter Dam maine Sw.---to the beginning. The sd. land was due by Trans. of 7 psons., 16 April 1683.

Jon: Golding	Edm'd. Reeves	Robert Bourne
Arthur Peirce	John Moor	Wm. Galel
	Wm: Peck	

p. 244. Maj. John Stith, an irregular tract of 236 Acres, 2 R., 16 po., in the Parish of Westopher & on the S. side of the Ja. Riv. Bounded: on the Northernmost Br.---crossing a Br. of the Northernmost Br.---crossing the maine Br. of the Northerne Br. & the most Westerly Br.---to 2 small Branches of the Northerne Br.

The sd. land was due by Trans. of 5 psons., 16 April 1683.

Alice Roomes	Isaac Maskew	Hen: Cheeseman
Roger Bell	Mary Brown	

p. 246. John Harris, 250 Acres, on the S. side of Ja. Riv., Parish of Wayonoake & on the E. side of Otter Dams. Bounded: on the Otterdames maine Sw.---crossing a round poynt ---to the beginning. The sd. land was due by Trans. of 5 psons.,

16 April 1683

Hugh Cardy	Robt. Barnes	Edm'd. Taylor
Tho. Holder	Robt. Huet	

p. 252. Mr. Jonas Liscomb, an irregular tract of 432 Acres, 1 R., 7 po., on the S. side of Ja. Riv., Parish of Westepher, on the Northern Br. Bounded: on the line of Maj. John Stith,

crossing a Br. of the Easternmost Br.---crossing a Br. of the Northerne Br.---to the Northerne Maine Br., to the beginning. The sd. land was due by Trans. of 9 psons., 16 April 1683.

Jon: Tucker	Tho: Lylly	Danll. Parker
Hen: Pott	Esw'd. Cooke	Tho. Rockwell
Margt: Jones	John Simpson	Tho: Scafe

p. 270. Mr. Daniell Higgdon, an irregular tract of 518 Acres, 1 R., 16 po., on the w. side of Ja. Riv., Parish of Westover. Bounded: at a corner poplar of Maj. Francis Poytherys standing upon the Middle Southern Br.---to Mr. Warradine---crossing the Hollow bush Br.---crossing the Middle Br.---to William Edmonds corner tree---upon the line of Maj. Francis Poytheris. The sd. land was due by Trans. of 11 psons.,

16 April 1683.   Gee: Horne   Tho. Jarvis
Mary Hilliard   Ann Dawes   Edw'd: Chiswell
James Smith   Tho: Murrow   Jon: Mayden
Benjamin a negro   Katherine Stone
Mary Whiting

    p. 272. William Wilkins, an irregular Tract of 265 Acres, 1 R., in the Parish of Westover & on the S. side of Ja. River. Bounded: at the corner of Richard Cairlike---crossing the Mill path---standing in Hangmans Neck--- on the head of Bridge Cr.---on Blands path. The sd. land was due by Trans. of 6 psons., 16 April 1683.
Robt. Hurd   Ann Cooper   John Yeo
Wm. Thomas   Mary Phillips   Edw'd. Spicer

    p. 273. Mr. John Hobbs, an irregular tract of 381 Acres, 3 R., 20 po., in the Parish of Wayonoake & on the S. side of Ja. Riv. Bounded: on the Ponns main Run & belonging to the land of Benja: ffoster---to a corner gum---crossing Swift Br.---crossing the heads of 2 small branches.

the line of Morris Rose --- to the Main Sw. --- in the fork of the Cattailes & Poll Run. The sd. land was due by Trans. of 8 psons., 16 April 1683.
Robt: Crimly   Sarah Guy   Hen: Vernon
Robt: Berry   Wm: Hilson   Rich. Prince
                   Susanna Wilmett   Jane Hopkins

    p. 274. Mr. Daniell Higdon & Mr. Roger Reese, an irregular tract of 264 Acres, 1 R., 13 po., in the Parish of Westover & on the S. side of Ja. Riv. Bounded: on the Lower Kings field Br. --- along the line of Richard Pace, crossing the upper Kings field Br., and the long poynt Br. --- to the line of Col. Edward Hill.

The sd. land was due by Trans. of 6 psons., 16 April 1683.
Robt. Hix   Robt: Slye   Ann Dawes
Phillip Row   Mary Cooper   Ren: Crickett

    p. 285. Mr. Alexander Davison, an irregular tract of 220 Acres, in the Parish of Westover & on the S. side of Ja. Riv. Bounded: a corner tree belonging to the land of Mr. John Drayton Jr. --- crossing Blands Path --- the line of Mr. William Wilbison --- to Richard Carrills corner. The sd. land was due by Trans. of 5 psons., 16 April 1683.
Edw'd. Byrd   Jon: Kellum   Eliz. Phillips
Sisley Brookes   Xpher Yeomans

    p. 303. Mr. Thomas Anderson, an irregular tract of 400 Acres, in the Parish of Westopher & on the S. side of Ja: Riv. Bounded: in the line of Capt. Robert Lucy --- crossing the Cattaile Maine Br. --- crossing Mr. Wallices path --- to the beginning. The sd. land is due by Trans. of 8 psons., 20 Sept. 1683.
Eliz. Kish   Valen: Taylor   Tho: Barrow   Wm: Sheffeild
Wm. Stock   Jon: Stewart   Joseph Fells   Tho: Barrel

p. 305. Mr. Henry Harmond, Mr. John Bushop (the margin & the Index have Bishop), 168 Acres, 3 R., 23 Po., in the Pish. of Wayenoake & on the S. side of Ja. Riv. Bounded: at a corner Pine belonging to the Land of Isaac Boybson --- the line of John Hobbs --- to Mr. William Wilkins --- on the head of Jacob Bayleys land

--- along the heads of Mr. Rich'd. Warrens and Mr. John Bushops lands. The sd. land was due by Trans. of 3 psons., 20 Sept. 683.

James Brown	Ed. Cooper	Peregrine Try

p. 328. Lt. Abraham Jones, 1217 Acres, in the Parish of Bristoll & on the S. side of Appomattox Riv., & bounded: on the S. side of Appomattox Riv., at the lower side of Maj. Gen. Woods lands, called the Indian Town lands --- near one of the branches of Rohowick --- in a peninsula made by the main run of the Southern Sw. --- to the uppermost corner of the sd. Fort lands. The sd. land was due by the Trans. of 25 psons., 20 Nov. 1683.

Geo.: West	Gilbert May	Steph: Buck
Rich: Rice	Hen: Price	Geo: South
Rich: Jones	James Badcock	Ed: Herbert
Jon: Price	Tho. Peacock	Alice Smith
Steph. Hall	Joan Dickson	Tho: ffloyd
Jon: Moor	Mary Thomas	Wm: Jones
Anne Hall	Peter Thompson	Rich: West
Eliz. Moor	Geo: Littlegood	Dennis Coniers
Giles Cook		

p. 329. James Jones, 734 Acres, 3 R., 24 po. in the Parish of Wyanoke & on the S. side of Ja. Riv. Bounded: at a place called Devils Woodyard --- the line of John Hobbs ---

crossing Pole Run --- on Cherry Br. --- to a corner white oak belonging to the land of Mr. William Harrison. The sd. land was due by Trans. of 15 psons., 20:9 ber:1683.

Matthew Holmes	Waller Hill	Jon: Wardon
James Munger	Jon: Hellen	Jon: Joyce
Hen: Bond	Wm. Novle	Tho: Jones
Wm: Prescot	Jon: Long	Tho: Cropey
ffra: Bradley	Jon: Baker	Rich: Staley

p. 331. Mr. John Williams, 842 Acres, 2 R., 25 po., in the Parish of Westopher & the S. side of Ja. Riv. Bounded: on the N. side of the Blackwater Main Sw. --- the corner pine belonging to the Land of Mr. Daniell Higdon --- to the line of Wm. Edmonds --- on a Br. that goes up to the head of the old Town --- crossing the head of Tanners Br. --- in the line of Col. Edw'd. Hill --- the line of Richard Pace. The sd. land was due by Trans of 17 psons, 20 Nov. 1683.

Rich'd. Hamer	Sarah Kitmore	Antho: Bow
Geo: Adams	Tho: Pattison	Jona: Elizer
Bartho: Swinboarne	Roger ffiffett	Ann Turner
Chester Atkins	James Rowland	Jon: Newel
Geo: Archer	Hugh James	Jane Long
Susan Mills	James Mills	

p. 332. Mr. Benja. Foster, 833 Acres, 1 R., 20 po., in the Parish of Wayonoake & on the S. side of Ja. Riv. Bounded: --- at White Medow, and runeth thence along Thomas Chapells line --- to the line of Mr. Pawl Williams --- to Wards Cr. --- to the Mill Path --- crossing Poles Runn and the Mill Path --- on the line of James Jones --- to Cherry Br. --- to Capt. Archers Corner --- to the line of Col. Edward Hill. The sd. land was due by Trans. of 17 psons., 20 Nov. 1683.

Rich'd. Gardner	Tho: White	Rich'd. Gant
Ed: Sadler	Isa: Ablesone	Ed: Butler
Ed: Cranage	Tho: Sayer	ffrs: Barcley
Xpher Hammond	Wm. Denson	Natha: Corder
Wm. Spackford	Ed: Hartwel	Hen: Symonds
Tho: Kirk		Wm: feldome

p. 335. Maj. Francis Poytheres, 1250 Acres, 2 R., 30 Po., in the Parish of Jordans, on the S. side of Ja: Riv. Bounded: a corner Poebery belonging to the Land of Sampson Ellis --- crossing the Great Sw. and Horne Br. to a corner Poplar standing in the Middle of Southern Br. --- to the line of Mr. Henry Batt --- to the heads of the sd. Poytheres, Mr. John Woodley & James Mumfords lands --- to the heads of the sd. Poytheres and to the dry bottom run ---. The sd. land is due by Trans. of 25 psons., 20 Nov. 1683.

Sarah Henley	Morgan Welch	John Lawrence
Eliz. Hayes	Roger Horner	Jon: Cole
Symon Rouse	Rich: Thornbury	Jon: Rubye
Jon: fflud	Tho: Wood	Jon: Auborne
Jen: Genway	Jane Graveley	Jon: Cooper
Geo: Bell	Wm. Wood	Jos: Marsh
Geo: Crosland	Wm. Arnold	David Haynes
Eli: Brown	Wm. Sarson	Tich'd. Hind

p. 336. Adam Morris, an irregular tract of 200 Acres, on the S. side of Appamattuck Riv. & in the Parish of Bristoll. Bounded: Mounteys Neck, beginning at a corner oake of Thomas Lowes --- Mounteys Neck Sw. The sd. Rich'd Bruce, Tho: Toolye, Jon: White, Barth: Horton.

p. 337. Col. Edward Hill, 980½ Acres, in Westover Parish & on the S. side of Ja. Riv. Bounded: 600 Acres thereof are bounded as in the Patent 13 Oct. 1652, to one James Warrodine, deserted & for want of seating; the other 380½ Acres contingent to the 600 Acres, in the sd. pish & on the sd. River, bounded: by a corner tree of the Lands of Bycars on the N. side of the Great Road --- in the line late sett out for Mr. ffrancis Poytheris --- to a hickory corner tree of Mr. Poythers --- "upon a line of Roger Tilmans land along James Bin fords Line --- to the line of Robert Abernathby" --- to a corner white oake of Abernathy, Wallice & this land. The sd. land was due by an orde of the General Court at Jas. Citty for 600 Acres, 28 Nov. 1682 & for Trans. of 12, 20 Nov. 1683.

Dor: Bradley	Jon: Wright	Geo: Hilliard
ffra. ffinch	ffra: Shelson	Tho: Branstone
Jen: fflood	Wm: Gage	(These are all the names under the Pat.)

p. 339. Peter Wycke & John Lenear (the margin: Lanier.) 1482 Acres, 3 R., 24 po., in the P(ar)ish of Westover & on the S. side of Ja. Riv. Bounded: at a corner that divides Wm. Pebbles & Thomas Chappells --- crossing a Br. of the Otter Dams and James Jones Path --- to a corner white oake belonging to John Harris --- crossing Henry Weysh Path --- crossing the Piny Slash --- crossing the head of the Birchen Sw. The sd. land was due by Trans. of 30 psons., 20 Nov. 1683.

Howel James	Bryan Smith	Jon: Sherney
Jon: Gold	Jon: Lumpton	Jon: Shaw
Margt: Sinckler	Jen: Pasmore	Sarah Cole
Tho: Bagwel	Tho: Gent	Wm. Hayward
Wm: Wayder	Tho: Jennings	Ellen Hayward
Walter Collins	Alex. Maly	Jon: Kendal
Benj: Bulmer	Oliver Symonds	James Hows
Jen: Weaner	Walter Chiles	Xpler. Branch (as is)
Wm. Gill	Hen: Tutton	Jon: Gibson
	Jon: Matham	

p. 381. Henry Smith, 748 Acres, on the Warrick Sw. Bounded: on the S. side of the Sw. --- crossing Mr. Henry Witches path --- crossing the Notaway Path --- crossing Tonotura Path --- crossing Warrick Maine Sw. --- to the line of Hugh Lees. The sd. land was due by Trans of 15 (not named), 26 April 1684.

p. 387. ffrancis Leadbeter, 548 Acres, 32 po., in the P(ar)ish of Bristoll & on the S. side of Appamatick Riv. Bounded: at a place called Worrockhock --- at land of Hugh Lee, crossing Alder Br. The sd. land was due by the Trans. of 11 (not names), 26 April 1684.

p. 407. William Harrington, 250 Acres. Bounded: at a corner pine belonging to the Land of Capt. Thomas Busby --- to Joshuah Meachams corner --- on Myry Meadow. The sd. land was due by the Trans. of 5 (not named), 21 Oct. 1684.

p. 466 (possibly belongs here.) John Scott, 100 Acres, granted to John Smith dec'd., lately Escheated, Inq., before Col. John Page, Esch'r. of Chas. City Co., Jury 9 Aug. 1683 & now granted to the sd. John Scott, 20 April 1685.

p. 469. Hercules fflood, 296 Acres, in the P(ar)ish of Jordans & on the S. side of Ja: Riv. Bounded: nigh the blackwater --- to the line of Mr. Henry Batt. The sd. land was due by Trans. of 6 (not named), 20 April 1685.

p. 488. James Jones, 364 Acres, in the P(ar)ish of Westove & on the S. side of Ja: Riv. Bounded: on the E. side of the Mill Path --- in the line of Capt. Archers --- to the line of Thomas Chappells --- the line of Col. Edward Hill. Part of this land, 141 Acres, was granted to Thomas Tanner by Patent 27 Nov. 1657 & assigned to the sd. Jones. The other 223 Acres is Kings Land. The 364 Acres is due by Trans of 5 psons., (not named), 4 Nov. 1685.

p. 489. John Elles, 464 Acres, in the Parish of Bristoll & on the S. side of Appamattuck Riv. Bounded: at a corner black oake belonging to the land of Mr. Abraham Wood Jones

(as is) and running thence along the sd. Jones his Lyne ---
to the Maine River. The sd. land is due by the Trans. of 10
psons. (not names), 4 Nov. 1685.

p. 490. James Smith, an irregular Tract of 67 Acres,
in the P(ar)ish of Weynoake & on the S. side of Ja. Riv.
Bounded: at a corner pine belonging to the land of James
Jones standing on the Lyne of John Hobbs. The sd. land was
due for the Trans. of 2 (not named), 4 Nov. 1685.

(The following 3 Patents are from the No County Indes.
The first 2 are given as a list only for information: Bk. 7,
p. 464, Richard Washington, at the main Blackwater. Bk. 7,
p. 503, George Lawrence, on the Blackwater in the upper Parish
of Nansamond. Note: the latter obviously does not belong to
those of this County of Chas. City, but is included in the list
to show the extent of the Blackwater.

(p. 510. possibly belongs in the Chas. City area.
Nicholas Wyatt, 115 Acres, scittuated near his dwelling house
in Mcht. Brandon P(ar)ish. Bounded: a corner betwixt Capt.
Wyat & Elizabeth Wheeler, orphan --- in Ralph Rachells line
--- betwixt his & Mr. Wallis's home. The sd. land was due
by Cadwallader Mackerry   James Hollis   Wm: Bourne)

p. 512. Mr. John Terry, 750 Acres, between Chipoakes and
Wards Cr., & bounded: on the N. side of a Br. --- between the
sd. Terry & ffrance Ree --- corner tree betwixt him & John
Roackes --- inter Rookes & Mr. Goods --- to a pine, Henry
Armstrongs corner tree; the land is now in possession of
Edward Green I belonging to an orphan of Wm: Shorts; ten by
Shorts line in Mr. Richard Clarks line --- corner tree betwixt
him & John Wilkinson --- to Capt. Wyatts corner tree. The sd.
land is due by Trans of 15 psons, 27 April 1686.
Wm. Wilson   Jno. Johnson   Rich. Webber
Jeremiah Jones   Susan Wyer   James Fry
Mary West   Joane Trefry   Wm. Adams
Wm. Jands   Wm. Mott   3 Negroes
(All that are names under the Patent.)

p. 531. Nicholas Wyatt, son & heir of Anthony Wyatt
late of the P(ar)ish of Jordans, dec'd., all that plantation
called Chaplins, on the S. side of Ja. Riv., P(ar)ish of
Jordans, and bounded: a line now or late of Col. Edward Hill,
that runs into Masons --- down to Bickers Cr., containing
361 cres.. The plantation of Chaplins was due to the sd.
Nicholas Wyatt as Eldest son & heir of Anthony Wyatt, who
dyed lately, and by reason of (the)burning of the house, the
Patent which was granted to one Chaplin was lost, and the
original at the Secretary's Office could not be found. 13
Oct. 1686.

p. 542, (No County Index, which may belong here.)
Francis Ree, 330 Acres, Bounded: on the N.W. side of upper
Chipoakes Cr. --- corner tree betwixt Mr. John Terry & the
sd. Ree. The sd. land was due by Trans of 7 psons, 30
Oct. 1686.

p. 535. Robert Bowling & Mr. Daniell Monaley, 347
Acres, in Bristoll P(ar)ish & on the S. side of Appamatok

Riv. Bounded: at a corner black oake of Mr. Tobt. Bowling ---. The sd. land was due by Trans. of 7 (not named), 30 Oct. 1686.

p. 535. Mr. Edward Birtchett, 230 Acres, Bristoll P(ar)ish & on the N. side of the Maine Blackwater, bounded: --- to Mr. Robt. Tuckers corner ---. The sd. land was due by Trans. of 5 psons., 30 Oct. 1686.

Edmund Vickary
James King   Wm. Cooper   Thomas Morin
                Richard Newman

p. 536. Mr. Samuel Tatum, 803 Acres, in Bristoll P(ar)ish at a place called Warrockhock. Bounded: corner marked tree belonging to the land of John Smith --- up the Great Br. ---. The sd. land was due by Trans. of 17, (not named), 30 Oct. 1686.

p. 543. Henry Gauler (Mr.), 400 Acres, on the Blackwater called Rowman, in Bristoll P(ar)ish. Bounded: on the Blackwater. It was formerly granted to Patent to Hugh Lee, 20 April 1680 & deserted & since granted to Mr. Henry Gauler, by the General Court, 16 Oct. 1686, & is due by Trans of 8, 30 Oct. 1686.

Wm. Canter   Wm. Jones   Jeremy Johnson
Jane Rhodes   Hanah Ellis   Susan Herd
               Jonas Kieth   Jane Willis

p. 543. Mr. Henry Gauler, an irregular tract of 265 Acres, 1 R., 13 po., Westover P(ar)ish & on the S. side of Ja:Riv. Bounded in Lower Kings field Branch --- crossing the Upper Kings field Br. & the Long Point --- to the line of John Williamson --- crossing the Blackwater Path 20 po. to John Williamsons corner --- to the line of Col. Edward Hill. The sd. land was formerly granted to Mr. Dan. Higgon & Mr. Roger Reeve, by Patent 16 April 1683 & deserted & granted to sd. Gauler by order of the General Court, 16 Oct. 1686 & for Trans. of 6 psons., 30 Oct. 1686.

Tho: Charles   Phoebe Jones   Jno: Wyn
Griffin Paul   Tho: Williams   Alice Pierce

p. 546 (may belong here.) Mrs. Sarah Williams, 750 Acres, formerly granted to Edmond Richards, escheated, Inq. before Capt. ffrancis Page, Dep'y Esch'r. of Chas. City Co., Jury 3 Nov. 1684 & now granted to Mrs. Sarah Williams, 1 Feb. 1686/7.

p. 553. Mr. Charles Goodrich, 550 Acres, in Westover P(ar)ish & on the S. side of Ja. Riv. Bounded: at the line of Danll. Higdon --- to lines of Wm. Edmunds & John Williams. The sd. land was due by Trans. of 11 psons. (not named), 20 April 1687.

p. 554. George Pace, 600 Acres, Westover P(ar)ish & on the S. side of Jas. Riv. Bounded: at a corner pine belonging to land of John Williams --- crossing the Blackwater Path --- crossing the Reedy Br., --- in Capt. Lucies line. The sd. land was due by Trans. of 12 psons. (not named), 20 Apr. 1687.

p. 564. (may belong here) James Bisse, 150 Acres, formerly granted to Mr. Arthur Harwood dec'd. & lately escheated, Inq. before ffrancis Page, Dep'y. Esch'r., Jury 10 June 1685, & now granted to Capt. James Bisse, 20 April 1687.

p. 575. John Reeks, 320 Acres, on the N.W. side of Upper Chipoakes Cr. Bounded: at a tree betwixt the sd. Reeks & Doctor Terry ---. The sd. land was due by Trans. of 7 psons., 20 April 1687.
John Keys	David Pibes	Hen: Clark
John Woodnell	Tho. Scot	Ralph Haynes
	Alex. Snart	

p. 583. Mr. Thomas Wyn, 280 Acres, Jordans P(ar)ish & on the S. side of Ja: Riv. Bounded: at the lower corner tree of Mr. John Wynns land --- to Balles Cr. --- along Maj. Poytheres line --- in Mr. Batts line. The sd. land was due by Trans. of 6 psons., 20 April 1687.
ffrancis Hughes	Jno. Light	Wm. Gawry
Jane Strangler	Wm: fforest	Edw'd. Hughes

p. 633. William Whittington, 250 Acres, in Bristoll P(ar)ish on the S. side of the Northernmost Blackwater. Bounded: at a great corner Lyne belonging to the land of John Gollighty --- on the line of Isaack Colson. The sd. land was due by Trans. of 5 psons., 23 April 1688.
James Tuthill	Xpher. Adeer	Tho. Gothan
Geo: Bass	Math. Roope	

p. 654. Henry Alley, 390 Acres, in Bristoll P(ar)ish, on the Northernmost Br. of the Blackwater. Bounded: at a corner black oake belonging to the land of Willm. Vaughan --- to Henry Crondon's corner --- to John Evans corner gum --- along the lines of Mr. Rich. Jones. The sd. land was due by the Trans of 8 psons., 23 April 1688. Rich Jones Edw'd Richard
Anne Collings	Tho: Charles	Roger Norris
Avis Collings	John Besse	Maria a Negro

p. 657. Thomas Busby & Mary his wife, daughter & heirs of Simon Simons, 539 Acres, on the S. side of Jas. Riv., part in Winoak & part in Westover Parrishes. Chas. City Co., & bounded: at the Branch of Powell's Cr. called Reedy Bottom Br. --- it crosseth a branch of fflowerdy hundred Cr. --- dividing the sd. land from lands now or late of William Harryson, thence along the Lands now or late of John Hobbs --- thence along John Poythres line North --- which divides this from the lands of the sd. Poythres West --- to the Reedy Bottom Br. ---. The sd. land was due the sd. Thomas & Mary, 359 Acres thereof are within the ancient bounds possessed by Simon Simons, grandfather of the sd. Mary, and 150 Acres, the deserted lands late of James Ward dec'd., by order of the General Court, Jas. City, 17 Oct. 1687, & the residue. 30 Acres, between the aforesd. line of Hobbs & Poythres & 350 Acres for the Trans. of 11 psons., 26 April 1688.
John Rogers	Francis Pitt	John Lake
Andrew Cob:	Patrick Johnson	Thomas Leech
Anthony Holder	Robert Long	Jeffry Cond
Adus Strong	Roger Gras	

p. 707. Roger Tilman, 1060 Acres, Chas. City Co., Parish of Bristoll & on the S. side of Appamattock Riv. at a Place known by the name of Moneuaneck. Bounded: at the mouth of the Great Br. & runs up that Br., being nigh the line of Thomas Loe's land S.E. -- thence N. crossing a great Cr. & a Beaver Pond --- to a corner white oak & maple standing on Moneua-neck main Runn ---. The sd. land was due by Trans. of 2 (not named), 20 April 1689.

p. 708. James Thweat, Sr., 125 Acres, Chas. City Co., in Bristoll Parish, on the S. side of Appamattock Riv. Bounded: at a corner black oake belonging to the line of Mr. Henry Blatt, thence E. & by N. ½ N. 68 po., to a corner gum being the line of Edward Birchett, thence on his line S. by E. --- to Birchett's corner, thence N. The sd. land was due by Trans. of 3 (not names), 20 April 1689.

p. 709. Reynard Anderson, 328 Acres, in Bristoll Parish, Chas. City Co., on the S. side of the first Blackwater Sw. Bounded: at the Water sourse of the Sw., thence S. --- along marked trees, falling on a Br., thence down that Br. --- thence up along the water course of the sd. Sw. ---. The sd. land was due by the Trans. of 7 psons., not names, 20 April 1689.

p. 714. James Mumfort, 50½ Acres, in Westopher Parish, Chas. City Co., on the S. side of Jas. Riv. Bounded: at two red oakes upon Mr. John Woodlifs Line & running S. --- thence along Maj. ffrancis Poyth r(e)ss Line E. --- to a red oak in a Branch of dry bottom, thence along the sd. Mumforts S.E. Line N.W. ---. The sd. land was due by trans. of 1 (not named), 20 April 1689.

Book 8

p. 25. Jno Gillom, 261 Acres, in Parish of Bristoll & on the S. side of Appamattick Riv. Bounded: at a point of Rocks and extending into the woods S. --- to the line of Hugh Leadens Land, thence on Leadens Line N. & by E. --- to a pare tree on the Riv., thence up the Riv. ---. The sd. land was due by trans. of 6 (not named), 20 Oct. 1689.

p. 39. Mr. John Scott, 74 Acres, in Chas. City Co., Parish of Bristoll & on the S. side of Warreck Maine Sw. Bounded: at a corner white oak standing on the Maine Sw. & run(n)ing S.W. & by S. --- to a corner white oak crossing Warreck Sw., N.W. by N. --- to a corner poplar standing on Wanoak Maine Sw. ---. The sd. land was due by trans. of 15, 21 April 1690.

Jno. Roberts	James Vaughan	Mary Vaughan
Tho. Joquis	Barth. (?) Turner	Tho. Voss
Sarah Newton	Jno. Meadowes	Abrah. Read
Tho: Collins	Eliz: Willis	Wm. Holsworth
Ja. Cook	Jno. Nicckols	Jer. Watts

p. 38. Thomas Chamberlin 856 Acres, Chas. City Co., Parish of Bristoll & on the S. side of Appamatuck Riv., and

at a place known by the name of Rihoweck. Bounded: at a
corner black oak belonging to the land of Mr. Abraham Jones
& running to one Wm. Jones his line W. ½ S. --- to a corner
white oak standing on the Oterdam Riv., th(en) up that run
--- to a corner pine by a Great Beaver Pond, the(en) down that
Br. --- to Mr. Abraham Jones his corner, then on his Lines N.
--- crossing Rehoweck Maine Br. ---. The sd. land was due by
trans. of 21 April 1690 of 18 psons. (not named.) Under
the Patent: 18 rughts by Mr. John Soan as he is assignee of
Wm. Hunt. Certified by E. Chelton Cl.

    (p. 55, No County Index, may belong here. Thomas Wynne,
on Blackwater, 659 Acres. Bounded: at a tree of John Wallices
Land & along a Line of Hercules Flood, S. --- a tree of Maj.
Fra: Poythris dec'd. --- to the mouth of Bland's Br. ---
along the Great Sw. --- on the land of Jno. Williams, thence
S. --- sd. Wallice dec'd. S. W. ---. The sd. land was due
by trans. of 14 (not named), 21 April 1690.)

    (p. 55, No County Index, may belong here. Nicholas
Robinson & Nicholas Durell (originally written Duwell, and
corrected), on Blackwater, 289 Acres. Bounded: a corner
tree of Mr. Ja: Wallice, dec'd., & S. S.W. along the Line
of the sd. dec'd. --- to the 2nd Sw. to the hog pen Br. ---
along the meand'rs of the Run of the Ashen Br. N. --- to the
mouth thereof, thence through the 2nd. Sw. to the corner
tree of Hugh Lees Sr. Land ---. The sd. land was due by
Trans. of 6 psons., 21 April 1690.

Jno White	Sarah James	Rich'd. Wheelehouse
Robt. Middleton	Jno: Farmouth	Rich'd Tunstall)

    (p. 57, No County Index, may belong here. Hercules
Flood, on the Blackwater & on the E. side of Ready Br.,
1254 Acres. (Bounded:) having the land of William Harris &
Adam Taplie for bounds thereof along the E. side of land of
Capt. Henry Batts & the main woods & the Ready Br. on the
W. side & the Ready Br. & the land of ffrancis Pothress on the
N. side --- to the corner tree of the Land of Wm. Harris &
Adam Taplie, thence along Wm. Harris Line --- along the line
of Harris & Taplie --- to a black oak by the side of a knowll
th(en) N. --- to a corner tree of Capt. Henry Batt --- to
the further (as is) side of the Ready Br. --- to Maj. ffran.
Poithris Land ---. The sd. land was due by Trans. of 26
psons., 21 April 1690.

Jane Johan	Tho. Kay	Edwd. Willoughby
Wm. Powell	Henry Nowell	Jane Nowell
James Lock	Jno. Nowell	Jervis Kay
Wm. Rudder	Tho: Rudder	Robt. Allin
Jarvis Wrack	Joan Scarlett	Robt. Whaley
Dorothy Rooke	Robt. Lock	Sarah Ridley
Robert Smith	Wm. Long	Robt. Mallard
Robert Crod	Robt. Joy	Sarah Moat
	Rich'd. Games.)	

    p. 60. Mr. Henry Randolph, Mr. James Cock, John Golightly
& Solomon Crook, 647 Acres, Chas. City Co., Parish of Bristoll
& at a place known by the name of the Second Sw. Bounded:
at a corner white oak belonging to the land of John Sturdivant, thence W. by N. --- crossing the Second Sw. --- to

Mr. Sturdivants corner white oak, thence on his line N.N.W. ½ W. ---. The sd. land was due by Trans. of 13 psons., 19 Feb. 1690.

Wm. West	John West	Jno. Baxter
Mary Pedum	Paul Vaudin	Thomas Wolly
Mary Woply	(or Vandin)	Peter Prior
Clare Vaudin	Robt. T: (as is)	
Robt. Man	Ann Welly	
	James Miller	

p. 71. Mr. James Cock, Jno. Butler & Wm. Low, 1684 Acres, Chas. City Co., at a place known by the name of Moncusoneck. Bounded: at a corner white oak belonging to the Land of Jno. Evans & Roger Tillman & running on the lines of theirs N.E. --- crossing Cattail Br. to a corner pockrey, th(en) E.S.E. --- crossing the upper Nottaway Path ---. The sd. land was due by trans. of 34 psons., 21 April 1690.

Wm. Barker	Alice Cockin	Rich'd. Rogers
Joane Barker	Jame Popper	Wm. Cocken
Benja. Lucas	Nath. Goldin	Robt. Boakley
Robt. Case	Phill. Incues	Margt. Ballingster
James Brown	Mary Read	An: Phipes
Jame Palmer	Mary Lowman	Mary Benet
Sam Ward	Jno. Jones	Jno. Tophler
Eliza. Luce	And: More	Eliza: Toats
Tho. Wilkinson	Jer: Brookes	Margt. Robinson
Tho. Swift	Mary Chapham	Cha: Mackartes
Hen: Clenck	Eliner fford	

p. 74. John Herbert, 1215 Acres, Bristoll Pish, Chas. City Co., at or near Moncosaneak. Bounded: of a corner white oak of the Land now or late of Rog:r Tillman on the W. side of Hatchers Run, thence W. --- to Hatchers Run aforesd., thence down that Run --- passing through Moncasaneak Mayn Sw. ---. The sd. land was due by Trans. of 25 psons., 20 April 1690.

Miles Hockley	Ja: Webster	Andrew Wray
Jno. Deering	Tho. Steele	Will: Mills
Jno. Lockley	Andrew Jeffers	Tom, Sambo, Moll,
Abraham Elmer	Mary Lockley	Negroes
Susanna Elsby	Jno. Sampson	Adam Roe
Emanuel Robins	Dorothy Howard	
Sarah Mills	Rich: Panbooke	

p. 75. John Herbert, 287 Acres, Bristoll Pish, Chas. City Co., & on the S. side of Apamatock Riv. Bounded: at a corner gum on the sd. Riv. belonging to John Ellis and thence on his line S.E. by S. --- crossing a Br. --- crossing a Great Br. of Powhipanock & crossing Powhipanoo Mayn Br. ---. The sd. land was due by Trans. of 58 psons. Note: 30 rights by Edw'd. Chiltons Cert. to Mr. David Crafford, dated 2 May 1685. Also

Wm. Jeffrey	Abraham Jackson	Timo. White
Bernard Moore	Mary Neill	Jaquis J(o)nson
Peter Elliott	Edward Hinton	Andrew Beale
Ja: Watson	Edward Cary	Robtert Haines
Wm. Janet	Tho: Yates	Nath: Carter
Rich: Harwood	Millicent Baker	Eliz: Greene
Mary Clayton	Joan Wilson	Ambros Page

David Andrews   Edwd. Poisson   Ja: Parker
Hen: Wootton   Tho: Pirkins   The Patent is dated
Randall Crayford   Hannah Hall   21 April 1690.

p. 75. John Evans, 818 Acres, Bristoll Parish, Chas. City Co., adj. to 557 Acres of other lands granted to the sd. Evans by Patent 22:9ber:1682. Bounded: on the E. side of the Southern Run, thence crossing the sd. Run W. ---. The sd. land was due by trans. of 17 psons., 21 April 1690.

Anth: Tarkin   Ja: Appleby   Peter Treake
Susanna Hall   Wm. Weaver   Andrew Cosby
Adam Rugsby   Jno: Roper   James Thornton
Jno. Carver   Tho: Hambleton   Robert Ellis
Jane More   Joan Relfe   Antho: Hux (?)
                 Grace & Judith, negroes

p. 76. Henry King & Thomas Parham, equally to be divided between them, 824 Acres, Bristoll Parish, Chas. City Co., at or near Monosaneak. Bounded: at a corner white oak of the land now or late of Roger Tillman on the side of the Great Br., thence up that Br. --- thence up Tillmans line S. --- to the Cow Br., then down that Cow Br. along by Lows corner tree & still down that Br. until it falls into Moncasaneak Main Run. then down that run to the mouth of the Great Br. aforesd., then up that Br. to the beginning. The sd. land was due by Trans of 17 psons., 21 April 1690.

Jane Rookeley   Ann Jones   Jno: Turner
Sarah Wharton   Jno: Nasbee   Robert Rookeley
Geo: Hewlett   Tho: Dickenson   David Morgan
Adam Earley   Robert Savadge   Robert Creede
Wm. Moroan   Jno. Turner   Jane Hughes
                   James Ashton   Guy a Negro

p. 76. Henry Wall, 275 Acres, Bristoll Pish., Chas. City Co., and (bounded:) at or near Rahowick, at a certain hickory corner tree of the lands now or late of Maj. Cahmberlin, thence E. --- crossing a run or branch --- one of the lines late of Col. Wood now or late of Maj. Chamberlin, thence along the line of marked trees S.W. ---. The sd. land was due by Trans. of 6 psons., 21 April 1690.
Harry, Sambo, Ruth, Tom, Moll, Ned, Negroes.

p. 77. Nicholas Overbee the Younger, 323 Acres, Bristoll Pish., Chas. City Co., at ir bear Rahowick. Bounded: at a corner of the lands late of Col Wood which also is a corner of the lands late of Abraham Jones, and thence along the sd. Jones marked line E. --- to a pine by the side of a run or branch, thence down that Br. --- where it falls upon one of the lines of Henry Wall, crossing that Br., then along that line E. --- where it falls upon one of the lines of the land late of Col. Wood aforesd, then along that line N.E. ---. The sd. land was due by Trans. of 7 psons., 21 April 1690.

Anth: Ragsdale   Jno: Pawlett   James Holines
Robert Wilson   Sarah Howes   Ruth Wigmore.
Tho: Gilson

p. 77. Mathew Marks, 556 Acres, in Martin Brandon Pish. Chas. City Co., & bounded: at a corner gum near Wards run and thence up a line of old marked trees of the lands late of Edward Richards S. --- to a gum, thence by a line of the lands now of Mr. Blighton S. by E. --- a marked white oak on the sides of the aforesd. Wards run, thence up along the water coves (or cones) of the sd. run ---. The sd. land was due by Trans. of 11 psons., 21 April 1690.

Tho: Wells
Jno: Simpson
Rich: Kewis
Wm. Webster
Robt. Wood
Adam Good
Edwd. More
Diana & Robin, Negroes
Jane Whitby
Wm: Wright
Waltin Long

p. 77. Thomas Chapell, 904 Acres, Chas. City Co. Bounded: at a red oak in one of the lines of Robt. Bollin and along that line of old marked trees E. --- to a white oak of the aforesd. Bollin, then E. ---. The sd. land was due for Trans. of 19 psons., 21 April 1690.

Wm. Gordon
Jno. Throgmorton
Sarah White
Rebecca Edward
Tom (blurred) & Dick, Negroes
Tho: Ramsey
Jno: Welch
Aron Wood
Ja: Bellamy
Tho: Hannon
Abrah: Doughtye
Jane Emerson
Robt: Lander
Jane Wood
Jno. Wharton
Tho: Maples
Adam Wells
Roger Holt

p. 78. Adam Taply & William Harryson, 1078 Acres, Jordans Parish, Chas. City Co. & on the S. side of Jas. Riv. Bounded: at a hickory in one of the lines of Maj. Poythres Land, thence W. --- to a red oak near Nich: Whitmors line, N. ---. The sd. land was due by Trans. of 22 psons., 21 April 1690.

Ja: Allen
Ja: Lewis
Jno: Whiting
Tho: Osborne
Ruth Everett
Elsue (or Elssie Snow
Tho: Randall
Hudson Isham
Robt. Norton
Richard Mallard
Tho: Oxly
Robert White
Geo: Rudder
Wm: Rosse
Geo: Nelson
Jno: Willoughby
Joshua Royston
Antho: Scarlett
Edwd: Hutchison
Sarah Moore
Rich: Isham
Robt. Wells

p. 80. Eliza. Wallis & Mary Wallis, daughters & coheirs of Mames Wallace dec'd., 567½ Acres, Chas. City Co., formerly granted to Joseph Johnson by Patent 14 Sept. 1642 & by the sd. Johnson assigned to Jno. Banister, 7 June 1645 & by sd. Banister bequesthed to his wife by will, 12 Oct. 1660, but in case she married in Va. the same to come to John Judseth and was lately found to escheat from the wife of the sd. Jno. Banister of Chas. City Co.: Inq., before ffrancis Page, Dep'y. Esch'r. of the sd. Co. & a Jury 3 Dec. 1685 & now granted to the sd. Eliza & Mary Wallis, 21 April 1690.

p. 86. Henry Talley, 350 Acres, Chas. City Co., Bristoll Pish & on the S. side of Appamattux Riv. Bounded: at a great rock on the Otterdams r. & running N. by W. --- to a corner black oak standing in the Line of Wm. Jones then on his line W.N.W. --- standing on a branch then up that branch leaving Jones his line S. --- as the sd. branch winds to a corner black oak, the(en) E. 92 po. to a corner poplar standing in the Otterdam Br., then down that Br. ---. The sd. land was due by Trans. of 7 psons., 23 Oct. 1690. Sambo, Jack Rosse, Harry, ffranck, Judy, Dick.

p. 86. Richard Ligon, Saml. Tatom & Wm. Tempell, 1022 Acres, Chas. City Co., Bristoll Pish. & on the S. side of Appamattuck Riv. at a place known by the name of Warreek Sw. Bounded at a corner white oak on the sd. Sw. belonging to the Land of Jno. Ledbetter, running on his line N.W. to the Land of Jno: Scott, th(en) on his line S.W. --- crossing Warreck Br. to a corner pine, th(en) W.E. --- to a corner white oak standing in Warreck Main Sw. ---. The sd. land was due by Trans. of 21 psons, (not named). Not dated. Marginal Note: Never issued. Teste W. Edwards, Sec'y. Cur. Note under the Patent; The Gov'r. refused to sign the Pat."ffer that part of it said on ye South side of the main Blackwater Sw. ---" (Note by the Editor: the words Blackwater Sw. are not in the test; probably Warreck Sw. was intended.)

p. 104. Capt. Roger Jones, 347 Acres, Chas. City Co., Bristoll Pish. & on the S. side of Appamattox Riv. Bounded: at a black oak of Mr. Robt. Bollings land th(en) along his lines S.W. by S. --- to a corner pine standing in a great slash, th(en N.E. by N. ---. The land was formerly granted to Mr. Robert Bolling & Mr. Danl. McNaley, and then deserted & since granted to the sd. Jones by order of the General Court, 16 April 1690 & due by Trans of 7 psons., 23 Oct. 1690.
John Johnson. Sambo, Nick, Guy, Tony, Wassa, Sam., Negroes

p. 106. Mr. Robert Bolling, 400 Acres, on the Blackwater, called by the name of Rownam, Chas. City Co., Bristoll Pish., & bounded: from a corner marked pine standing on the Blackwater, th(en) S. by E. --- to the Reedy Br. --- to the Blackwater ---. The sd. land was due: formerly granted to Hugh Lee by Patent 20 April 1680, deserted, and since granted to Mr. Henry Gauler by Patent 30 Oct. 1686, deserted & now granted to the sd. Bolling by order of the Generall Court, 16 April 1690 & by Trans of 8 psons., 23 Oct. 1690.
Jno. Sanders   Lucy Festervill   Jno: Richardson
Robt: Holmes   or Testervill   Eliza: White
Tho: Robins   Rebecca Branch   Tony a Negro

p. 111. Mr. John Bannister, 1730 Acres, Chas. City Co., Bristoll Pish. & at a place known by the name of Hatchers Run. Bounded: at a poplar standing on a Br. of the sd. Run & running thence W.W.W. --- to a corner poplar standing in a great Br. of Hatchers Run, thence down that Run ---

p. 112

thence crossing the Run S. by E. --- to a corner ash tree on Hatchers Main Run, thence up the sd. Run S.W. & by W. --- to the mouth of a small run & thence up that run S. by E. --- to a great pcell. of Rock, thence N.E. --- crossing Hatchers Run ---. The sd. land was due by Trans of 35, 23 Oct. 1690.
Abraham A Negro   Giles Waters   Jno: Ellis
John Spell   Elizabeth Hollis   Jno: Eggerton
Anne Berry   William Standback   William Southaway
Sarah Pollard   Humphry Hix   Hester Vaughan
John Alee   ffrancis Hill   Negro Jenny
Antho: Hasket   Mary Drew   ffrancis Goard
Gewen Berry   Sanders Bruce   Wm. Price
Wm. Taylee   Martha Occandon   Jno. Davis
Wm. Brown   Wm. Price   Nath: Dison

Jno. Thomas   Robt. Aston   Wm. Davies
Gabriel Arthur   Tho: Gent   Ellin:r Vaughan
                     Sam. Bupton   Phillis Millington

    p. 123. Mr. Edward Holloway, 819 Acres, Chas. City Co., & on the S. side of Jas. Riv. Part of this land, 250 Acres, granted to William Arrenton, bounded: at a corner pine standing on the Mirey Meadow & running th(en) W. --- to a stake in the Great Meadow, th(en) N. by E. --- th(en) on the line of Joshua Meacham N.N.W. --- to a corner gum standing in a Br., th(en) N.E. ---. Of the sd. land, 569 Acres was due to the sd. Holloway by Trans. of 12, 23 Oct. 1690.

Jno: Daniell   Tho: Lambert   Robt. Elson
James Nicholls   Adam Bush   Sarah Bush
Wm. Roberts   Jno: Welsh   Abrah: Rethden
Jone Phillips   Tho: Maples   Jno: Sanders

    p. 125. Samuel Jourdan, 450 Acres, 1620. This Patent was abstracted by N. M. Nugent, "Cavaliers and Pioneers," p. 226, for which see.

    (p. 127, from the No. County Index, listed for reference Maj. Arthur Allen, 200 Acres by the edge of the Blackwater; p. 174, to same, I. of W. Co., 170 Acres; p. 175, to same, 525 Acres.)

    p. 149. William & Richard Vaughan, 281 Acres, Chas. City Co., Bristoll Pish & on the W. side of Moccense Neck Main Sw. Bounded: at a corner ashe tree belonging to the Land of Thomas Low and running thence W. by N. --- to a corner black oake standing on Hatchers (run), thence down the sd. Run as it tends to Moncuseneck Main Sw. & thence up the sd. Sw. ---. The sd. land was due by Trans. of 6 psons. Not dated.
Jno: Bull   Eliz. Price   Dick, Tom, Name, & Pelighey(?).

    p. 173. Henry Batt, 700 Acres, on the branches of Baylies Cr., in Chas. City Co., towards the S. side of the head of the sd. Cr. Bounded S. by E. by James Warrendines Land, commonly known by the name of High Peake, and now in the occupation of Mr. Wm. Ditty and Robert Langram, E. by N. along the woods having the W. & S. branches running through the sd. Land. The sd. Land was formerly granted to Mr. Wm. Batt by Patent 22 April 1670, deserted, and since granted to the sd. Henry Batt, by order of the General Court, 27 April 1691, and due by Trans. of 14 psons., 20 Oct. 1691.

Wm. Sharpe   Dorothy White   John Sawer
Anne Mary (as is)   Tho: Bucher   Saml. Anderson
  Children of Thomas   Antho. Morley   (All that are given.)
  Bushell   Math. Hurst

    p. 174. Wm. Knott, 216 Acres, Chas. City Co., & bounded: at a marked oak on the Chipkes Cr., thence N.W. by N. ---. The sd. land was formerly granted to John Wanpoole by Patent, 26 April 1682, deserted & since granted to the sd. Knott by order of the General Court, 15 April 1691, & by Trans. of 5 psons., 20 Oct. 1691.

Hester Downes   Wm. Bently   Jno: Underwood
Mary Parlett   Wm. Grea

p. 211. Christopher Addison, an irregular tract of 265 Acres, 1 R., 13 po., Chas. City Co., Westover Pish. & S. side of Jas. Riv. Bounded: on the lower Kingsfeild Br. --- on the line of Richard Pace, crossing the upper Kingsfeild --- on the Line of John Williamson --- on the line of Col. Edw. Hill ---. The sd. land was formerly granted to Danll. Higdon & Roger Roose, Patent 16 April 1683 & by them deserted & afterwards granted to Mr. Henry Gauter (or Ganter) by order of the General Court. 9ber:16th:1686, who now patented the land & since granted to the sd. Addison by order of the General Court, dated 16 Oct. 1691 & by Imp. of 6 psons., 20:8ber:1691.

| John Nicholls | Judeth ffranklin | Robert Roye |
| La: Stephens | Tho: Walkman | Hen: Jells |

p. 218. Solomon Crooke, 89 Acres, Chas. City Co., Bristoll Pish., viz., beg. at a corner tree belonging to the Land of Robert Burdges and runs thence on the line of Mr. Coleman S.E. & by E. ½ E. 126 po. to a corner white oak by Baleys Meadow, thence S. by E. --- on the line of Hugh Lee --- thence W. by N. --- thence N.E. --- to the place it began. The sd. land is due by the Imp. of 2 psons., 29 April 1692.
Timothy Redding   Eliz. Clarke

p. 244. Ralph Jackson & Joseph Maddox & John Dagles, 784 Acres, Chas. City Co., Bristoll Pish., vizt., beg. at a corner white oak standing on a samll Br. falling into Mounseneck Maine Cr. & runs thence W. 20 po., crossing Wildcat fall down to a corner pkrey, thence W.N.W. --- thence N. by W. --- thence N.E. --- thence N. by W. --- thence W.N.W. --- thence N. --- thence E. --- thence S.E. --- thence N.E. by E. --- thence S.E. --- thence E. --- thence E.N.E. --- crossing Wildcatt fall down, thence S.E. by E. --- thence S. --- thence S.W. by W. 126 po. to 2 corner pines standing on our center Br., thence down that Br. --- to the beginning. The sd. Lane was due by Imp. of 16, 29 April 1692.

| Geo. Hatton | Rich. Longwell | 11 by cert. from |
| Eliz. Kendall | Pomply & Gay (or Jay) | Wm. Edwards, 6 (-) 1689. |

p. 244. Hugh Lee Sen:r & John Barler (or Barlow or Barton), 530 Acres, Chas. City Co., Pish of Jordans, vizt., beg. at a corner pockrey of the afsd. Lees old Land & runs thence S. --- thence E. --- thence S. E. & By E. --- thence S.E. by S. --- thence E. --- thence S.E. 7 by 6 po. to a corner ash tree in an Ashen Br., thence down that Br. as it trends to the mouth --- thence N.N.E. --- thence N.W. & by N. --- thence W.N.W. --- thence N. by W. --- thence N.W. by W. --- thence S. S.W. on John Smith('s) Line and crossing the Second Sw. 110 po. to his corner, thence on his Line & Lees W. 406 po. to the beginning. The sd. land was due to Hugh Lee & Jno. Barlor by Imp. of 11 psons., 29 April 1692.

James Catthill	Xopher Adgar	Robt. Heath
Rich Bas	Geo. Bas	Tho. Goton
Mary Harnson	Jno. Borrow	Jno. Crump
Geo. Packar	Mathew Rope	

p. 267. Richard Turberfeild, 200 Acres, on the S. side of Appamattuck Rev., Chas. City Co., Bristoll Pish. At a

place named Monkey's Neck., beg. at a corner white oake of Thomas Lowes line and runs thence N.E. by E. --- thence N.W. by W. 242 po., crossing the Maine Monkey's Neck Sw. --- thence N. by W. --- thence W.S.W. --- thence S.S.E. --- thence S. --- thence S.E. 106 po. to the LIne of Thomas Lowe, thence along the sd. Lowes line N.E. by N. 148 po. to the beginning. The sd. land was formerly granted to Addam Morris by Patent 20 Nov. 1683 & by him deserted for want of seating & now granted to sd. Turberfeild by order of General Court, 26 April 1693, and is due by Imp. of 4, 29 April 1693.
John Jones   Abraham Lucket
William Canter   Richard Wheeler

  p. 315. William Low, 674 Acres, on the s. side of Appamatux Riv., Chas. City Co., Bristoll Pish., at a place called Moneasanock, viz., beg. at a corner white oake & runs thence S.E. & by E. crossing the first & second branches --- thence S.W. crossing Persimon Cr. --- thence W. & by S. --- thence W.N. W. 12 po. to Monensanock Maine Sw., thence crossing the Maine Sw. N. & by E. 2 deg. Ely. --- thence W. & N. 26 po. to a corner gum standing in a Small Br., thence N. thence N.E. &

       p. 316

by N. 254 po. to the first station. The sd. land was formerly granted (to) Thomas Lowe, the sd. Wm.'s father, Patent 20 April 1682 & by him deserted & since granted to the sd. Wm. Lowe, son of the sd. Thomas, by order of the General Court, 20 April 1693, & for Imp. of 14 psons., (not named), 20 April 1694.

  p. 367. ffrancis Ledbeter, John Ledbeter & William Jones, 300 Acres, Chas. City Co., Bristoll Pish., Vizt., beg. at a corner white oake standing in the fork of Warwick Maine Sw. & runs thence N. by E. 72 po., crossing the Breat Br. of Warrocks to a corner black oake, thence S.E. by E. --- thence S.E. 322 po. to 2 corner white oaks standing on the maine Br. of Warrock Sw., thence up the Maine Sw. as it trends to the place it began. The sd. Lane is due to them for Imp. of 6 (not named), 29 April 1694.

  p. 368. George Pasmore, 93 Acres, Chas. City Co., Jurdons Pish., vizt., beg. at a corner black oake standing on the line of William Jones and runs thence on his line N.W. --- thence E. by N. --- thence N.E. --- thence S.E. by E. ¼ Ely. 31 po. to the Line of Mr. Henry Batts, thence on his line S. by E. 26 po. to a corner pine on the line of John Wallice S. ---thence S. W. ½ W. 166 po. to the place it began. The sd. land was due by Imp. of 2 psons, 20 April 1694. Catherine Clark   Jane ffurbush

  p. 368. Thomas Parram, 70 Acres, Chas. City Co., on the Blackwater Sw., beg. at a corner pine on the sd. Sw. & runs thence N. by W. along the line of James Thweat 50 po. to his corner, thence on the line of John Clay W. by S. 99 po. to the Line of Henry King, thence on his Line S. by E. 140 po. to the Main Sw., thence down the Main Sw. as it runs to the place it began. The sd. land was due for Imp. of 2 psons., 20 April 1694.
Jno. Kelsey   Wm. Anderson

p. 369. Robert Hickes, 600 Acres, Chas. City Co., Bristoll Pish., & on the S. side of Appamatuck Riv., vizt., beg., at a corner white oake belonging to the Land of John Eavans and runs thence S.S.W. --- thence S. --- thence S.W. by S. --- thence S. --- thence S.W. --- thence S. --- thence S.S.W. 58 po. to the line of Mr. James Cock, thence on his line W.N.W. 185 po., crossing the second Sw. to a great pine and a Round Pond, thence N.E. by E. --- thence N.N.W. 26 po. and N.W. 68 po. & N.W. by N. 3/4 W. 15 po. to a corner pine on the line of John Evans, thence on his line N. --- to the place it began. The sd. land was due by Trans. of 12 psons., 20 April 1694

Roger Jones	Tho: Miller	Jno. Binley
Richard Griffith	ffra: City	Wm. Kerney
Geo: Clayton	Jno. Wright	Eliz. Clark
Jno. Prichard	Richard Bates	Wm. Dradge

p. 370. John Hamblin, 265 Acs., C.C. Co., S. S. of Jas. River., Westopher Parish, vizt., beg. at a marked black oake, being the corner belonging to the Land of Richard Carlislle and runs thence N.E. & by E. 200 po. to a corner black oake, thence S. 32 po. to a corner black oake, thence S.E. by E. 46 po. cros(s)ing the Mill Path to a corner Spaniah oake; thence S. by E. 100 po. to a corner black oake standing in Hangmans Neck, thence S.W. by S. 52 po. to a corner black oake standing on the head of Bridges Cr., thence down the Cr.. S.S.E. 60 po. to a High Point, thence S. E. 20 po. to a corner white oake standing on the sd. Wilkins ancient marked line, thence W. by N. 32 po. to a corner pine thence still along the sd. Wilkin's ancient line W. & by S. 230 po. to a former corner being a white oake standing on B. lands Path, thence bounding on the head of Alexander Davisons Land N. 7 deg. E. 194 po. to the place it began. The sd. Land being formerly granted to William Wilkins by Pat. 16 April 1683, by him deserted & since granted to John Hamblin by order of Gen'l. Ct., Jas. City, 26 April 1693 & for Imp. of 6 psons. (not given), 20 Apr. 1694.

p. 371. Thomas Chappell, 423 Acres, C. C. Co., S.S. of Jas. Riv. on the Herdam Sw., vizt., beg. at a corner pine on the sd. Sw., being the corner of the Land of Thomas Smith & runs on his line N.N.E. 3/4 E. 85 po. to a corner white oake, thence N.W. 202 po., cros(s)ing a great Br. to a corner white oake on the N. side of the sd. Br., thence by that Br. as it trends to a corner black oake N.W. 40 po. and S. W. 146 po. cros(s)ing the Atterdam Sw. to a corner live oake, thence up the Atterdam Sw. as it trends to a corner pine by a small Meddow, thence S. W. & by S. 78 po. to a corner pine, thence E.S.E. 232 po. to a corner pine, thence S.E. 74 po. to a corner black oake, thence S.S.E. 128 po. to a corner black (oak?), thence E. 74 po. to the line of Thomas Blunt, thence on Blunts line N. by E. 66 po. to the Atterdam Sw., thence crossing the Sw. N.E. 3/4 E. 24 po. to the place it began. The sd. Land was due unto the sd. Thomas Chappell by Trans. of 9 persons, 20 April 1694.

Negroes

Buck	Mingo	Sarah
Doe	Gerald	Abell
Santall	Moreton	Sus

p. 411. Capt. Henry Batt, 700 Acs. upon Branches of Baylys Cr. in C. C. Co., towards S. S. of the head of the sd. Cr., bounded as followeth: S. by E. by James Warading's Land called High Peake and now in occupation of Mr. William Ditty & Robert Langman, E. by N. along the woods having the Westerly & Southerly Br. run(n)ing through the sd. Land. The sd. Land was formerly granted to Robert West by Pat. 2 Aug. 1652 & by him deserted & to Capt. Henry Batt by order of Gen'l. Ct. 22 Apr: 1695 & for Imp. of 14 psons., 24 April 1695.

Michael Maxfeild	Mary ffenns	Mary Pain
Jno. Donklin	Robert ffenly	Geo. Keeble
Robt. Bushell	Mary Tedder	Rich'd. Langly
Marey Worley	Jno. Kenedey	Rich'd. Wallis
Mary Woods	Jno. Ellett	

To same, same p. & date, 270 Acs., Parish of Bristoll on S.S. of Appamattock Riv., C. C. Co., being an irregular tract containing all the wast(e) Lands betw. the Lands of Christopher Woodward on the Riv. & the Land called Baylys, on the heads of the Land of Mr. John May's on the Southward, and the Lands in possession of James Hall to the N. & N.E. & bounding S. from a marked pohickory (tree) to Henry Newcombs corner tree, 66 cha. E. on the Lands called Baylies & Newcombs, S.E.S. 10 cha. & 9 linkes to a great marked pine S. by E. on the Land of Mr. Mays to his corner crossing, the path at Mayes that leads to Baylyes, 47 cha., thence W. by S. crossing the head of 2 branches to an old corner marked tree near Hafford 49 cha., thence N.N.W. to a corner shrubbed oake near the plantation called Hafford 33 1/2 cha., thence N. by W. over the run called Hafford & run(s) to the Kings road 32 cha., thence N. W. on the Land of Woodwards toward the Riv. & N. & N.E. on the Lands now in possession of James Hall; the sd. Lands were part of the Patent of 870 Acs. to Sam: Woodward by the Patent 20 Apr. 1680, & deserted & to Capt. Henry Batt, by order of Gen'l. Court 22 Apr. 1695 & for Imp. of 6 psons., 24 Apr. 1695.

Mat. G. Miller	James Harris	Tho. Cook
Jno. Jones	Tho. Stanner	James Brown

p. 440. John Bonner, 346 Acs., C. C. Co., Parish of Weynoake, S. S. of Jas. Riv., vizt., beg. at a corner pine standing on the line of Joseph Meatchamp & a small Br. & runs thence N.N.W. 60 po. to a corner pine on Mr. Wallis his line, thence by line E.N.E. 118 po. to a corner pine and N. 1/4 W. 212 po., to a corner pine, thence N.E. 120 po. to a corner black oak, thence S.E. 1/4 E. 364 po. to a corner pine, thence E. 80 po. to a corner black oake, thence S.E. 320 po. to a corner black oake, thence the line of Edward Hollaway thence his lines N.W. 456 po. & W.S.W. 150 po. to a corner white oake standing on a small Br., thence down the branch as it trends to the place it began. The sd. 346 Acs. were due John Bonner by Imp. of 7 (not named) 21 Apr. 1695.

p. 441. George Passmore, 220 Acs., C. C. Co., on the S.S. of Jas. Riv., vizt., beg. at one head line of the Land of Mr. Robert Thucker & runs by head line of S.E. 42 po. to his corner pine, thence E.S.E. 60 po. to William Jones by his corner black oake, thence on the sd. Passmores own line E. by N. 71 po. & N.E. 63 po. & S.E. by E. 1/4 E. 31 po. to a corner pine on the line of Mr. Batts, thence on his line N. by W. 262 po. to Robert Burtchiles corner pine standing on the line of Coll. William Byrd Esq., thence by his line S.W. by S. 304 po. to the place it began. 220 Acres were to George Passmore by Imp. of 5 (not named), 21 April 1695.

Book 9

p. 2. Capt. Wm. Randolph, 2926 Acres, C. C. Co., Parish of Wiynoake, on a Sw. named Pigion Sw. on the S. S. of Jas. Riv., vizt., beg. at a corner black oake on the S. S. of said Sw. & runs thence S. S. W. 126 po. to a corner black oake, thence S. S. E. 200 po. crossing a Seedy Br. to a corner pine, thence S.E. 188 po. to a corner black oake, thence S.W. 90 po. to a corner hickory thence W. crossing a Meadow Br. 206 po. to a corner black oake, thence S.S.W. 466 po. to a corner black oake, thence S. & by E. 180 po. crossing a Meadow Br. to a corner black oake, thence E. crossing a Br. & the Main Pigeon Sw. 448 po. to a corner black oake, thence 390 po. to a corner pohickory, thence E. 83 po. to a corner oake, thence N.E. & by N. crossing a Br. 272 po. to a corner black oake, thence N.N.W. 95 po. to a corner pohickory, thence N.E. 79 po. to the corner pohickory, thence N. 272 po. to a corner black oake, thence N.E. 76 po. to a corner black oake, thence N. 36 po. to a corner black oake, thence N.W. 34 po. to a corner pohickory, to a corner gum, thence W. by N. 220 po. to a corner pine standing on the sd. Pidgeon Sw. by several aterdancy(?), thence up the said Sw. to the place it began. The sd. Land was due for Imp. of 59 psons., 25 Oct. 1695.

Tho. Competon	Peter Prout	ffra. Cleavley
Nicholas May	(or Pront)	Hugh Davies
Wm. Jessup	Jane Borer	Jno. Herbert
Andr. Martin	Robt. Beazley	Elira (or Eliza)
Sam Courser	John Witt	Harrison
Jno. Gates	Joan White	Negro Nell
Walter Squire	Alice (--, as is)	Benetha Clause
Tho. Revill	Pat. ffosler	Anne Newton
Geo. Cocobill	Robert Covey	Rebecka Bollitt
Job (--, as is)	Jno. Edwards	Sam Wright
Tho. Lyborn	Gill ffucket	Mary Jones
Rich'd Wheelhouse	Tho. Mathews	Owen Jones
Tho. Merrit	Wm. Warren	John Morris
	Jno. Evans	16 Negroes &
	Henry Baltamore	4 Negroes

p. 71. Capt William Randolph, 2926 Acs., C. C. Co., Parish of Weynoake & on a Sw. known by name of Pigion Sw., on the S. S. of Jas. Riv., vizt., beg. at a corner black oake on the S. S. of the Sw. & runs thence S. S. E. 226 po. to a corner black oake, thence S. S. E. 200 po. cros(s)ing a reedy Br. to a corner pine, thence S. E. 188 po. to a corner black oake, then S. W. 90 po. to a pohickory, thence crossing a Meadow Branch 206 po. to a corner black oake, thence S.S.W. 466 po. to a corner black oake, thence S. & by E. 180 po. crossing a Meadow Br. to a corner black oake, thence E. crossing the Br. & the Main Pedgion Sw. 488 po. to a corner black oake, then N. then 390 po. to a corner pohickory, thence

E. 23 po. to a corner black oake, thence N. E. & by N. cros(s)-ing a Br. 272 po., to a corner black oake, thence N.W. 95 po. to a corner pohickory, thence N.E. 79 po. to a corner pohickory thence N. 272 po. to a corner black oake, thence N.W. 34 po. to a corner pohickory, thence W. N. W. cros(s)ing Black Sw., 24 po. to a corner gum, thence W. by S. 270 po. to a corner pine standing on the said Pedgion Sw. by several Otter Dam(s?), thence up the sd. Sw. as it trends to the place it began. The said Land was due for Imp. of 59 psons. (not named, but see p. 2), 15 Nov. 1696.

  p. 85. Robert Bolling, Gent., 300 Acs., C. C. Co., at the head of Walter Brooks 160 Acs., purchased of John Howell, who purchased of Natha. Tatem and runs E. along the head of Natha. Tatem(s) land 60 cha. then S. into the woods 80 cha., from whence it runs W. 150 cha., thence N. to the head of John Bakers Land 80 cha. and then E. to the place it began. The land was formerly granted to Walter Brooks who joined the same with other Lands in one Patent of 460 Acs., 12 March 1654 (see note at end) and deserted and since granted to Robert Bolling by order of Gen'l. Ct. 22 April 1697 & for Trans. of 6, 29 Oct. 1697.

Guy	Walter	Dick
Jack	Jane	Nan

(Note: C. & P., 298, Walter Brooks, 460 Acs., 12 March 1654, Bk. 3, 303. In Bristoll Parish, 160 Acs. described & 300 Acs. not described & only 2 of 6 Trans named. It is difficult to know if the 2 belong to the 160 or 300, but it says 6).

  p. 87. Instance Hall, 215 Acs., C. C. Co., S. S. of Jas. Riv. in Bristoll Parish, vizt., beg. at a corner pine belonging to the Land of Mr. Robert Bowling and runs thence W. by S. 178 po. to a corner black oake, thence S. by W. parting this survey & James Hall 230 po. to a stump called Woodward corner, thence E. by N. 146 po. to a line of Dan.'ll Sturdem, thence on his line N. 98 po. and N. N. E., 140 po. to the place it began. The Land was due for Trans. of 5 (not named) psons., 29 Oct. 1697. Note at bottom: "Rights Wanting."

  p. 125. John Martin, 307 Acs., on South side of James Riv., C. C. Co., Parish of Waynoke, a place called Otterdams at a corner white oake of John Harris' Land and runs thence along John Harris' Line N.E. 240 po. to John Harris' Corner being a black oake, thence S.E. & by E. 200 po. to a corner black oake, thence S.W. 245 po. to the Otterdam Main Sw. to a corner live oake, thence up the Sw. W. N. W. & N. W. 200 po. to the place it began. It was formerly granted Richard Williamson by Pat. 16 April 1683 (Pat. Bk. 7, p. 237, etc.) & by him deserted & to John Martin by ord: of Gen'l. Ct. 24 Oct. 1695 & by Imp. of 7 psons., 28 Oct. 1697.

Sarah Johny	jno. Doby	Rich'd Sparks	Tho. Joyner
Tho. tivey	Nes (as is)	Harry	

(2 others scratched out)

  p. 149. Nich: Overbey, 365 Acs., C. C. Co., Bristol Parish, beg. at the black oake side line to the sd. Overbeys land being a tract of 323 acres formerly taken up & Patented by him, the sd. line being a W. 27 deg. S. line 89 po. and runs then S. 15 deg. W. 104 po. to a pine by a slash called the round ponds, thence S. 50 deg. W. 60 po. to a Western Wading Path at a red oake near the upper side thereof, then 24 deg. W. 166 po. to 2 black oakes and a pine at the head of a Br. on a point then 64 deg. W. 109 po. to Ralph Jackson's line at a small red oake, thence along the sd. Jacksons line W. 32 deg. 1/2 N. 2 po. to a white oake corner of sd. Jacksons Land, thence along the sd. Jacksons corner, thence N. 23 deg. E. 120 po. to a scrubbed black oake, thence N. 104 po. to a gum in a Br. of Rohoick in the line of Mr. Rich'd Jones, thence along the sd. Jones line E. 1 Deg. 1/4 N. 82 po. to the sd. Jones corner ash S. along red oakes and a pine by the head of a Br. of Rohoick, thence along the sd. Jones line N. 10 deg. 3/4 E. 65 po. to a hickory corner tree to the sd. Jones and henry Wall, then along the sd. Walls land N. 29 deg. 3/4 E. 17 po. to a small red oake corner of the sd. Walls at or near the Main Br. of Rohoick on a hill side, then along the sd. Walls Land E. 13 deg. 3/4 N. 13 po. to the Main Br. of Rohoick, then up the Main Br. of Rohoick along the sd. Overbeys old land S. by E. 116 po. to a pine, thence along the sd. Overbey's old land E. 27 deg. N. 96 po. to the 1st mentioned beginning. The Land was due Nich. Overbey for Trans. of 7 psons (not named), 26 Apr. 1698.

p. 156. Wm. Vaughan & Rich'd Vaughan, 281 Acs., C. C. Co., on Muncusneck (See Land Patent, Bk. 8, 244) Maine Sw., vizt., beg. at a corner oake tree belonging to the Land of Wm. Low & runs thence W. by N. 41. po. to a corner pohickory, thence S. 103 po. to a corner pohickory, thence W. by N. 80 po. & W. S. W. 60 po. to a corner pine thence S. W. 33 po. to a corner white oake, thence W. S. W. 168 po. to a corner pine, thence N. W. and by W. 42 po. to a dogwood bush, thence S. W. 44 po. to a corner black oake standing on Hatchers run, thence down that run as it trends to the mouth thereof to Mancusaneck Maine Sw., thence up the Main Sw. as it trends to the place it began. The Land was due by Imp. of 5 psons. (not named) 15 Oct. 1698.

p. 157. Hugh Lee Jun'r., 950 Acs., C. C. Co., Parish of Bristoll at Notway Riv., vizt., beg. at a corner black oake on the Riv. to the W. Side of a small Br. & runs thence into the woods N. 92 po. to a corner gum, thence N. E. 62 po. to a corner black oake, thence E. 166 po. to a corner black oake thence --- E. 48 po. to a corner white oake, thence N. E. 142 po. to a corner pohickory, thence E. N. E. 68 po. to a former white oake, thence E. & by S. 98 po. to a corner "Buttwood" tree, thence S. E. 40 po. to a corner black oake standing on a great Br. names Jones Hole Br. thence down that Br. as it trends to the mouth thereof, thence up the Notway Main River to the place it began.
The Land was due by Imp. of 19 psons., 15 Oct. 1698.
John Blag - 8 times   Mary at   Jack - a Negro
John Buckley - twice   Oreginall Brownes   John Martin
Tho. Hilton   Eliz. Long
John Wright & wife   Harbertt Duncomb
& child

p. 163. Mr. Richard Jones, 230 Acs., C. C. Co., Parish of Bristoll S. S. of Appomattox Riv., vizt., bet. at a corner pohickory belonging to the Land of Henry Wall & runs thence S. by W. 64 po. to a corner pine, thence W. 153 po. to a corner pine, thence N. W. & by N. 1/2 W. 26 po. to a corner black oake, thence W. & by N. 1/2 N. Lat. (?) po. and N. by W. 1/4 W. 39 po. to a corner pohickory, thence W. N. W. 121 po. to a corner black oake, thence N. & by W. 1/2 W. 30 po. to a corner white oake standing on the Western B. of Rohowicke, thence down that Br. as it trends to the mouth thereof, and thence down Rohowicke Maine Br. as it trends to Rohowick Line, thence on that Line S. E. 3/4 E. 156 po. to a corner pohickory, thence on the Line of Henry Wall E. & by S. 1/2 S. 182 po. to the place it began. The Land was due for Trans. of 5 psons, (not named), 15 October 1698.

(Joseph Perry, 150 Acs., No. Co., lyeing on Warrick Sw. & Meadow (See Land Patent Bk. 8, 367), Vizt., beg. at a corner black oake standing on the sd. Meadow parting this survey & the Land of Thomas Chappell and runs on his line E. by S. 284 po. to a corner pine, thence on Capt. Leusbys (?) line S. 1/2 E. 70 po. to a corner gum standing in Warrick Sw., thence up the sd. Sw. & Meadow to the place it began. The sd. Land was due by Trans. of 3 (not named) 6 June 1699. Note at foot of the Patent: 3 rights paid for Mr. Byrd as p. certificate.

p. 220. William Randolph, 2926 Acs., C. C. Co., Parish of Wyanoke & on Pidgeon Sw. & on S. S. of Jas. Riv. vizt., beg. at a corner black oake on the S. side of the sd. S. Swamp (as is) and runs thence S. S. W. 126 po. to a corner black oake, thence S. S. E. 200 po. crossing a reedy Br. to a corner pine, thence S. E. 188 po. to a corner black oake.

221

thence S. W. 90 po. to a corner hickory, thence W. crossing a Meddow Br. 206 po. to a corner black oake, thence S. S. W. 466 po. to a corner black oake, thence S. by E. 180 po. crossing a meddow Br. to a corner black oake, thence E. crossing a Br. & the Main Pigeon Sw. 448 po. to a corner black oake thence N. 390 po. to a corner pohickory, thence E. 83 po. to a corner black oake, thence N. E. & by N. crossing a Br. 272 po. to a corner black oak & thence N.N.W. 95 po. to a corner pohickory, thence N.N.E. 79 po. to a corner pohickory, thence N. 272 po. to a corner black oake, thence N. E. 76 po. to a corner black oake, thence N. 36 po. to a corner black oake, thence N.W. 34 po. to a corner pohickory, thence W.N.W. crossing black Sw. 24 po. to a corner gum, thence W. by S. 270 po. to a corner pine standing on the Pigeon Sw. by several tter Dams, thence up the sd. Sw. to the place it began. The Land was formerly granted to sd. W. R. by Pat. 25 Oct. 1695 (See Pat. Bk. 9, p. 2) & by him surrendered up & ref. to King Williams grant of 10,000 Acs. in sd. Co. on S. side of the black water to his Royal College of Wm. & Mary in Va. & to W. R., who has already satisfied the King by Trans of 59 psons (not named, but see above) 26 Oct. 1699.

(Henry Talley, Bk. 9, 224, No Co., 280 Acs., S. side of Appamatock Riv., in Bristolo Par. & below the lands of the sd. Tolley the Land of Peter Jones an orphan and now in pos. of Stephen Cock and the Land of John Ellis, beg. at a gum being a corner tree to the sd. Talleys ould Land and standing

on the S. side of Reedy Br. & run(n)ing W. 25 deg & 1/2 N.
12 po. to a gum being a line tree of the sd. Jones now in pos.
of the sd. Cock, thence along the sd. Jones line now in pos.
of sd. Cock W. 23 deg. N. 137 1/2 po. to a heap of marked
trees W. 266 po. to a white oake corner tree being one of sd.
Ellis' trees and 2 pines and a white oake and a red oake
marked about the corner tree, thence S. 33 deg. W. 42 po. to
2 white oakes in the fork of Reedy Run, thence down along
Reedy Run to a black oake, being the upper corner tree of the
sd. Talleys ould Land on Reedy Br., thence down along Reedy
Br. along the sd. Talleys ould Land to the first beginning.
The Land was due for Trans. of 6, 26 Oct. 1699.
Evan Evans   Nich: O Hatcher   Jone
Edward Evans   Sampson Harry   (all)

     p. 225. Ralph Hill, 176 Acs., C. C. Co., Martins Brandon
Parish, beg. at a pine by the side of the Southern Br. at
the lower end of the Meddow, on the poynt of a Ridge of Land
betw. 2 small Branches & run(n)ing thence E. 40 deg. S. 62
po. to a pine, thence N. 44 deg. 1/4 E. 85 po. to a red oake
by the horick pathe, thence N. 182 po. to a pine, thence N.
30 deg. 5/8 W. 32 po. to 3 pines, thence W. 37 deg. 1/4 N.
25 po. to a corner pine of the Land of Capt. George Blighton,
thence along the Land of the sd. Blighton S. 51 deg. 1/4 W.
56 po. to a marked Spanish aoke held by the sd. Blighton,
thence along the Land of the sd. Blighton W. 8 deg. S. 60 po.
to the Southern run at a poplar, thence up the sd. Southern
run or Br. to the first beginning. The Land was due for
Trans. of 4, 26 October 1699. Stephen Sampson Sr., Mary his
wife, & Jane & Stephen, children.

     p. 291. Bartholomew Crowder, 242 Acs., C. C. Co., Parish
of Bristoll, betw. Lands of John Ellis & John Herbert & Ellises
Cr. or Run, beg. at a pine upon the sd. Allilles Line & run(n)-
ing thence along the sd. Ellises line S. 76 deg. W. 200 po.
to a red marked oake & a Spanish aoke corner tree to the sd.
Ellis, thence along the line of Mr. John Herbert W. 10 deg.
& 1/2 N. 113 po. & 1/2 to a corner white oake in the line of
the Land of sd. Herbert on the side of a poynt by Elisses Cr.,
thence up along the sd. Cr. or run, including the same in the
bounds to a rock run & So. along it to another Br. called
poplar Br. comeing out of the Main Br. making a fork in the
same, thence up along the sd. poplar Br. to a great oake,
thence out into the woods N. 30 deg. E. 173 po. to a forked
red oake, thence N. 50 deg. E. 134 po. to a pine, thence N.
21 deg. 3/4 E. 44 po. to a black oak and 2 pines, thence 53
deg. & 3/8 E. to the beginning. The Land was due for Trans.
of 5 (not named) 17 Nov. 1700. Note under the Pat.: five
Rights paid for to me Audit R. Byrd.

     p. 298. Robert Bolling, 300 Acs., C. C. Co., Bristoll
Parish, vizt., beg. in the fork of Warwick Main Sw. and runs
thence N. by E. 27 2 po. crossing the great Br. of Warrocks
to a corner black oake, thence S. E. by E. 134 po. to a
corner pohickory, thence S. E. 322 po. to a corner white oake
standing on the main Br. of Warrock Sw., thence up the Main
Sw. to the place it began. The Land was formerly granted
to ffrancis Ledbeter, John Ledbeter & William Jones by
Patent 20 April 1694 (See Land Pat., Bk. 8, 367) & deserted
& since to R. B. by order of Gen'l. Gt. 15 Oct. 1701 & for
Trans of 6, 25 April 1701.

John Hill   Alexander Scott   John Johnson
Walter Edwards   Corn. Macon   Peregrin Fry

(Maj. Arthur Allen, Bk. 8, p. 127, No Co., 200 Acs., ---
formerly granted to Richard Washington by Patent, 20 April
1685 & deserted & granted to the sd. Allen, etc. The Land
was on the Blackwater.

From Bk. 9, No Co.: There are two patents described,
being on the S. side of the main Blackwater, No Co., the first
to Richard Washington and the second to James Allen; but there
is a question whether these lands were then in C. C. Co.
on the S. side of the James River, now Pr. Geo. Co., A third
is to Geo. Williamson; a 4th to Wm. Edwards and Arthur Allen;
5th to Col. Nath. Harrison & Hinsha Gillam; 6th of Arthur
Allen; 7th to Chas. Brige; 8th to Patrick Lashly; 9th to Wm.
Edwards; 10th to Tho. Blunt & 11th to same; 12th to Lt. Col.
Wm. Browne; 13th to Wm. Hunt; 14th to Abraham Evans; 15th to
Hinsha Gillam; 16th to Tho. Blunt; 17th to John & Arthur
Washington; 18th to Tho. Reeves; 19th to Robt. Smelley, Thos.
Giles, Joseph Bridger, Lewis Smelley & Wm. Smelley; 20th to
Geo. Pearse; 21st to Robt. Smelley, etc.; as 19; 22nd to
Rich. Holliman & so 23rd; 24th to Tho. Harnison & John Scott
& 25th to Wm. Williams. All of the several references are to
Bk. 9, pp. 325-519. In addition to Ben. Harrison, on the S.
side of Nottaway Riv., Bk. 9, p. 706.)

p. 337. Thomas Busby, 5400 Acs., C. C. Co., bew. Joseph's
Sw. & Jones hole otherwise called Barle Thorpe Cr. in new
rutland on the N. side of Nottaway Riv. about a mile or 1 1/2
mi. from the same begin(n)ing at 2 pines in a Br. called
Parting Br., which parts this land & the land of Mr. James
Minge Sen. & run(n)ing W. 42 deg. 1/2 & 1/8 N. 109 po. to an
heap of marked trees, then S.W. 95 po. & 1/2 to a white oake
& a gum by a Br. called Tim:o Readings Br.

338

in sight of the plantation where King lives, thence N. 24 deg.
& 1/8 W. 103 po. to a white oak & a black oake, thence W. 24
deg. & 1/8 S. 60 po. to a Little Br. near a black scrubbed
oake, thence N. 35 deg. & 3/8 W. 72 po. to a red oake, a
black oake & a white oake, thence W. 1 deg. 1/2 & 1/8 S. 83 po.
& 1/2 to an hickory sapling thence N. 9 deg. & 3/4 E. 84 po.
& 3/4 to a red oake & a hickory & 2 sapling black oakes, thence
S. 72 deg. & 1/4 W. 240 po. to a white oake by Joseph Sw.,
thence over the sd. Joseph Sw. S. 51 deg. 3/4 & 1/8 W. 32 po.
to the S. side of the sd. Sw., thence up Joseph Sw., S. 77
deg. 1/2 & 1/8 W. 41 po. to a white oake on the S. side of the
sd. Joseph Sw. S. 9 deg. & 3/4 W. 104 po. and 3/4 to an heap
of marked scrubbed black oakes, thence E. 1 deg. & 3/4 S.
114 po. to a red oake and a hickory, thence E. 32 deg. & 1/2
and 1/16 S. 66 po. to a hickory sapling, thence S. 43 degrees,
3/4 West 95 po. to 2 scrubbed black oake & an old marked black
oake, thence East forty degrees 3/4 and 1/8 S. 121 p. po. to
a standing hickory and a scrubbed black oake and an old marked
corner black oake, thence S. 33 deg. & 1/8 W. 82 po. & 1/2 to
a white oake, thence W. 1 deg. & 1/2 & an 1/8 S. 132 po. &
1/2 to a bending hickory & white oake, thence W. 10 deg. &

1/4 N. 74 po. to a black oake, thence N. 11 deg. & 1/8 W.
94 po. to a black oake over John Dobey's Br., thence N.W.
32 po. & 1/3 to a white oake by Dobey's Br., thence S. 66 deg.
& 1/2 W. 68 po. & 1/3 to a white oake, thence E. 67 deg.
1/2 & 1/8 S. 254 po. to 2 scribbed black oakes, thence S. 12
deg. 1/2 & 1/16 W. 88 po. to two white oakes by Little Houce
Meadow on Br., thence S. 19 deg. 1/2 & 1/8 W. 84 po. to 2
black oakes, thence W. S. W. 212 po. to a gum & 2 black
oakes

339

N. 100 po. to Ante Shurch alias Colechurch Br. in new rutland
being a Br. of Balethorpes Cr. or Jones hole at a whitewood
tree and down along Ante Shurch Br. to the mouth of the same S.
24 deg. & 1/2 W. 300 po., thence along Barlethorpe Cr. alias
Jones' hole S. 14 deg. E. 490 po. to a Spanish oake corner
tree upon the sd. Barlothorpe Cr. alias Jones' hole being a
corner tree between this Land & the land of Richard Gourd,
thence along the land of Richard Gourd N. 76 deg. E. 33 po.
to an hickory corner tree to the Gourd's land, thence along
the sd. Gourd's land E. 7 deg. 1/4 & 1/8 S. 26 po. to a gum
near a live oake Corner to the sd. Gourd's land, thence E.
54 deg. 3/4 to 1/8 S. 186 po. & 1/2 thence E. 32 deg. 1/2 &
3/16 S. 190 po. to a black oake, thence E. 10 deg. 1/4 &
1/8 S. 84 po. to a white oake, thence E. 51 deg. & 1/16 S.
56 po. to an hickory, thence E. 38 deg. & 3/8 S. 78 po., &
1/2 to a Spanish oake, thence E. 65 deg. 1/2 & 1/8 S. 71 po.
& 1/2 to a black oake, thence E. 21 deg. & 3/8 S. 218 po. to
a scrubbed black oake, in the low grounds by the foot of the
hills, thence S. 67 deg. & 1/4 E. 89 po. to a scribbed black
oake, thence N. 26 deg. & 1/4 E. 98 po. to a black oake, thence
N. 1/2 deg. W. 183 po. to a white oake & a red oake & 3
hickoryes, thence W. 72 deg. & 3/8 N. 228 po. to a black oake,
thence N. 9 deg. E. 47 po. to an hickory in the Line of College
standing by Joseph's Sw., thence along the College Line W.
1 deg. & 3/4 S. to the College Corner tree, being a black
oake 652 po., thence along the College Line N. 1 deg. & 3/4
W. 748 po., thence E. 1 deg. & 3/4 N, 88 po. along College
Line, thence E. 43 deg. & 1/4 S. along College Line 119 po.,
thence along College Line E. 1 deg. & 3/4 N. 560 po to a white
oake corner tree to the College land standing to Joseph's
Sw., thence up Joseph's Sw. N. 7 deg. & 1/2 W. 257 po. to the
mouth of Parting Br., or near the same, thence over the sd.
Joseph's Sw. and up Parting Br. N. 51 deg. E. 363 po. to the
begin(n)ing. The Land was due by imp. of 108 psons.,
(not named), 25 Apr. 1701.

378

Henry Jones, 400 Acs., C. C. Co., N. side of Nottaway
Riv. on upper side of Joseph's Sw., beg. at North of Joseph's
Sw. at the lower end of an island & run(n)ing thence to a
white oake and a hickory on the bank of the Cr. or gutt
of the Isl & thence N. & by E. 86 po. to a hickory and 2 red
sapling, thence N. 30 deg. W. 180 po. to a Spanish oake near
a meadow, thence W. 16 deg. N. 187 po. to a great pine by
the side of a meadow, thence W. 5 deg. S. 277 po. to 4 pur-
simon sapplins in a meadow, thence S. 23 deg. & 3/4 E. 30 po.
to 2 hickory sapplins, thence S. 15 deg. E. 36 po. to an heap

of sapplings by the side of an Indian feild, thence E. 12 po. to a greate Birch tree on the River on the lower side of a neck of land that makes out into the River a little above Tohinnk fyling place, thence down the River to the first beginning. The Land was due for transportation of 8 persons, 24 Oct. 1701.

Job Giles   Thomas Mitchell   Richard Williams
Simon Johnson
And three rights paid to Wm. Byrd, Esq., Auditor.

380

Capt. Francis Epps, William Epps & Capt. Littlebury Epps, 1000 Acs., C. C. Co., S. side of Worwich Sw. & N. side of Joseph's Sw., beginning at a white oake, a corner tree to the Land of John Scott, standing on the Worwich Sw. above the meadow and run(n)ing thence along the Land of the sd. Scott S. Wo & by S. 96 po. to a white oake and a pine & 2 red oakes along the land of the sd. Scott W.N. W. 94 po. to red oakes, thence N.W. 60 po. along the sd. Scott, to a white oake corner tree to the sd. Scott thence W. 148 po. to a black oake, thence N.W. 72 po. to a black oake, thence W. 62 po. to a black oake by a pond thence S. W. 322 po. crossing a great Br. to an hiccory, thence W.S.W. on 104 po. to a black oake, thence N.W. 99 po. to a black oake, thence S.W. 66 po. crossing Nunatora to a butterwood tree a little above the bridge over Joseph's Sw. upon the sd. Sw. & down along the sd. Sw. to 3 greate white oakes, being corner trees to the Land of Capt. Thomas Busby, thence E. & by N. 1/4 N. 60 po. to a red oake, thence N. 71 deg. & 3/4 E. 154 po. along the Lands of the sd. Busby to a black oake at an heape of marked trees, thence E. 22 deg. N. 348 po. to an hickory that stands by the meadow path that goes from Chr. Robinson's to Samuel Tatems, and thence E. 23 deg. & 3/4 S. 34 po. to the above sd. Busbys old corner "caled" the three oakes, thence E. 6 deg. & 1/2 N. 52 po. to the Worwich meadow at an hickory & so along the same course to the amin Run off the sd. meadow, thence up along the sd. meadow & the Worwich Sw., including the same in the bounds of the Land to the main Run of the Land to the begin(n)ing. The Land was due by trans. of 20 persons, 26 Oct. 1701.

Mathew Rane   John Spike   Mary Britton
Sam. Iles   Vincent Godfrey   John Edwards
John Gretion   Robert Gillereast   John ffan
Richard Owen   Martha Pattison   Avis Whiteker
Wm. Joyce   John Tucker   Dennis Cailer
Eliza. A. Gilson   Wm. Wooan   John Walker
                     Robert Matter   Jacob Johnson

382

Henry King, 400 Acs., C. C. Co., Parish of Bristoll, vizt., beg. at a corner pine standing on the S. side of Moncus Neck Cr. & runs thence S.S.E. 320 po. to 3 black oakes standing at the foot of Snow hill, thence S.E. 160 po. to 3 corner pohickorys, thence S.W. 160 po. to a corner black oake, thence N.W. 160 po. to three corner black oakes thence N. 12 deg. W. 436 po. to a corner white oake thence E. 84 po. to the beginning. The Land was due for trans. of 8, 24 Oct. 1702.

Jonathon Atkins   George Dance   Charles Hopton
Thomas Terry   Thomas Smuler   Thomas Lewton
Henry Wiggins   John Tillett

388

John Butler marrying Mary, one of the daughters of Mr. James Wallas, dec'd., in behalf of himself & the sd. wife Mary, who was the youngest daughter of the sd. Wallas & Eliz. A. Woodliffe, Widdow & eldest daughter of sd. Wallas, dec'd., 930 Acs., C. C. Co., to 1st & 2nd swamps of Blackwater & on the S. side of the 1st Sw. beg. at a white oake standing on the sd. S. side of the 1st Sw. of Blackwater, being 56 po. from the main Run of the Sw. on a N. 20 deg. E. course at a sweet gum & running thence along an old line S. 20 deg. & 1/2 W. 92 po. to three pines (about 1/2 cha., or po., from the old corner tree within the same), thence S. 13 deg. & 1/2 E. 280 po. (an old marked tree being a white oake - not closed), thence E. 2 deg. N. 83 po. & 4/6 to an old black oake, thence S. 15 deg. & 1/2 E. 128 po. to a pine burnt down in a small meadow over a Br., thence E. 2 deg. & 1/2 N. 108 po. to a pine, thence E. 31 deg. & 1/4 S. 27 po. to a small black gum (by the old black oake) thence S. 2 deg. & 1/2 E. 236 po. to a white oake over Hunts Br., thence E. 20 deg. S. 184 po. to a Spanish oake (a little within the corner), thence E. 47 deg. & 1/2 N. 184 po. to a gum standing on the Cr. or Beaver dam side of Blackwater Sw. (a great way within the old line), thence up along the 1st Sw. of Blackwater to the 1st beginning & including the Sd. Sw. to the main Run or Cr. within the bounds of the Land. The Land was due by trans. of 19 persons, 24 Oct. 1701.

Nich. Seale   Sarah Honnor   John Kempe
Mary Calcutt   John English   Vinc. Gotterple
Wm. Ball   Tho. Brockes   Rich. March
Edward Mitchell   Jos. Read   Wm. West
John Perry   John Brumfeild   Steph. Hix
Jeffery Hawkes   Tho. Chapman   Tho. Busby
                       George Walls

p. 390. Capt. William Hunt, 4342 Acs., C. C. Co., both sides of Nottaway Riv. & runs as follows: Beg. at a greate, old red oake standing by a sweet gum on the N. side of Nottaway Riv., being a corner tree of the College Land & running thence E. 3/4 of a deg. & 1/8 N. 260 po. to 2 black oakes, thence N. 3/4 of a deg. & 1/8 W. along the College Land 380 po. to a red oake, thence E. 3/4 of a deg. & 1/8 N. 92 po. to a black oake, thence S. 3/4 of a deg. & 1/8 E. 158 po. to a red oake, thence E. 10 deg. 1/4 & 1/8 S. 36 po. to an hickory, thence S. 23 deg. & 1/8 E. 766.

391

po. to a hickory thence S. 44 deg. & 1/2 W. 780 po. (this last course is good distance from the old line and within the same), to 3 white oake(s), thence S. 45 deg. & 1/2 E. 40 po. to a red oake and a pine, thence S. 44 deg. & 1/2 W. 146 po. to a red oake and a white oake, thence S. 7 deg. & 1/8 W. 44 po. to an old white oake by a black gum, thence S. 5 deg. 1/4 & 1/8 W. 26 po. to a white oake on the bank of Nottaway Riv. on the N. side of the Land marked with WH, being for the sd. Hunt's name, (is one of the corner trees of Liggon's survey) thence over Nottaway Riv. (which is about 10 po. wide) on a S. 168 deg. W. course to the bank on the S. side of the River, thence S. 68 deg. W. 15 po. to a white oake on the S. side of Nottaway Riv., thence S. 10 deg. 3/4 & 1/8 W. 109 po. to a black gum by a neadow on the side of a hill, thence S. 1 deg. 1/4 & 1/8 E. 43 po. to an hickory sapplin on the hillside by the meadow, thence W. 1 deg. 1/4 & 1/8 S. 29 po. & 1/3 to a red oake, thence W. 54 deg. 3/4 & 1/8 N. 194 po. to a red oake, thence N. 1 deg. 1/4 & 1/8 W. 180 po. & 1/3 to a hiccory sapplin, thence W 66 deg. 3/4 & 1/8 N. 83 po. & 1/3 to a red oake, thence W. 44 deg. 3/4 & 1/8 N. 45 po. to an old broken, topped, red oake (standing 2/3 of a po. to the left hand of this line), thence from the sd. red oake W. 22 deg. 3/4 & 1/8 N. 36 po. to a red oake in sight of a meadow, thence N. 3/4 of a deg. W. 73 po. & 1/3 to 3 red oakes, thence N. 35 deg. & 1/8 E. 414 po. to a white oake by the Cr. of the Island, thence along the meadoes of the Island Cr. W. 38 deg. N. 22 po. & N. 3/4 of a deg. & 1/8 W. 55 po. to a gutt comeing out of the S. side of Nottaway Riv., thence over the sd. Riv. & along the N. side to the beginning, including the Islands next adj. to the sd. Land in the sd. Riv. within the bounds, The land was due by trans. of 87 persons, 24 Oct. 1701.

John Pursell	Thomas Quin	Sarah Stuart
Rich. Moone	Step. Carder	Jno. Symons
Dan Donavaine	Geo. Williams	James Lough
Florence Donogline	Law. Loyd	John Conner
James Strich	Derby Bryan	Math. Kelley
Eds. Wheelan	Solomon Wills	Wm. Burton
Tho. Jones	Amy Loyd	John Hoohan
Geo. Dart	Martha Kenneday	Dan. Shine
Sarah Hambleton	Eliz. A. Philips	Wm. Armstrong
Rich. Caddy	Tho. Phelan	Rich. Butler
John Morish	Geo. Harry	John Drew
Cornel. Collaghan	Dorothea Jones	Edm. Cooslime
Kath. Hambleton	James ffury	Tim. Morgan
Rose Cotterell	Jno. Quinge	John Bray
Fred Jones	Garrett Purcell	Tim. Connell
John Rudd	Wm. Moone	Mathew Conier
John Roberts	Jno. Welsh	Wm. Donckin
Tho. Browne	Kath. Donoghone	Margt. Husey
Tho. Norpew	Robt. Pyke	Wm. Jones
Wm. Davis	Scipie Row	Jno. Carroll
John Norish	Mary Grant	Eliza Morgan
Dennis Risdane	Ja. Merradine	Lydia Sandes
John Browne	Jno. Barrey	David Herbert
Tho. Dunn	Thomas Trape	Dan. Kelley
Abra. Hobbs	Derby Raine	John Dowline
James Nowland	Jno. Lincey	John Jones
Mary Pliner	Louge Doran	Tho. Martine
Mary Moore	Wm. Angell	Mary ffarrell
	Law. Ketty	Simon Negro
		Robt. Glandon

p. 392. William Parkham, 450 Acs., on N. side of Nottaway Riv., in C. C. Co., in an Island between Monkese Neck, beg. at a birch by the brink of Nottaway Riv. & a white oake and a red oake sapplins and a holly tree & run(n)ing thence up along Nottaway Riv. to Monkese Neck Cr., thence up along Monkese Nick Cr. & a great meadow lying along the lower side (and coming out of the same) to a pine and a hiccory by the side of the sd. meadow 90 po. from the Riv. on a straight line, thence by a line of marked trees N. 10 deg. W. 188 po. to the Beaver dam Sw. which come(s) out of Monkese Neck Cr. and Fall(s) into the Indian Sw. at a maple & persimon, thence down along the sd. Beaverdam Sw. to 2 white oakes in a small neck between the sd. Beaver dam Sw. & a Br. coming out of the same & heading towards the sd. Parkhams Plantation, thence by a line of marked trees N. 40 deg. & 1/2 E. 43 po. to a scrubbed white oake sapplin over

393

the said Branch, thence down along the sd. Br. & the Beaver Dam Sw. to a marked tree in the sd. Sw. near the mouth where it empties into India Sw., thence by a line of marked trees S. 10 deg. E. 156 po. to the beginning. The Land was due by trans. of 9 persons, 24 Oct. 1701.
Mary Mandanell   Anne Winfeild   & 3 rights paid to
Mary Doughty   Elias Soper   Wm. Bryd, Esq.,
Rich. Longwell   James Thweat   Auditor.

     p. 393. Thomas Thrower & Georg Passmore, 680 Acs., C. C. Co., on the N. side of Jones Hole Sw. & the W. side of Cotefuroh Br., being a Br. coming out the sd. Jones Hole Sw., beg. at the mouth of the sd. Cotefuroh Br. by the lower Nottaway path run(n)ing thence up the sd. Cotefuroh Br. N. 28 deg. E. 333 po. to a maple in the sd. Br., thence W. 27 deg. & 1/2 N. 176 po. to a red oake, thence W. 8 deg. S. 140 po. to a red oake, thence S. 55 deg. W. 96 po. to a sapplin pine near Chewetos Br. being a Br. coming out of the sd. Jones Hole, thence W. 32 deg. N. 146 po. to an hiccory, thence N. 10 deg. W. 84 po. to the cherry orchard Br., being a Br. coming out of Jones Hole at a pine in the sd. Br., thence down along the cherry orchard Br. & Jones Hole Sw. to the beginning.

394

The Land was due by trans. of 14, 24 Oct. 1701.
Jone Jenkins   Mary Hilles Spencer Edward Dare
John Spell   Tho. Horn   Wm. Standback
Sarah Pollard   Humphry Hix   Jos. Passmore
Connie Berry   John Alee
Eliz. Duck   John Barlow
Robt. Barlow

     p. 394. Robert Hawthorn, 1400 Acs. C. C. Co., S. side of Nottaway Riv., beg. at a poplar at a persimon and a blackwalnut sapplins at the lower end of Oatcoes Meadow on or near the Bank of the Riv. by a red haw tree, thence up along Oatcoes Meadow S. 1/2 W. 90 po. S. W. 172 po. & W. by N. 98 po. to a pine on the sd. Meadows, thence S. W. & by W. 1/2 W. 112 po. to a black oake, thence S. & by W. 44 po. to Nottaway at a Spanish oake, thence up along Nottaway Riv. E. S. E. 80 po. & S. E. 30 po. to 2 white oakes on the Riv., thence S. E. 36 po. to 2 white oakes and a pine, thence N. 40 deg. E, 504 po. to a black oake, thence E. 21 po. to an hiccory and a black oake by the side of a meadow, thence along the side of

Meadow & S. W. of the same N. 43 deg. E. 120 po. to a white oake, thence the same course 458 po. to 2 white oakes, thence N. 51 deg. E. 78 po. over Cabbin Stick Sw. to a cupple of hiccory sapplins & red oake, thence according to the meanderings of Cabbin Stick Sw. E. 10 deg. N. 56 po. to a red oake and a black oake on the sd. Sw., thence N. 49 deg. E. 40 po. to a black gum and a

395

White oake sapplin & great pine on the top of the hill in barron, scrubby black oake land, thence N. 30 deg. E. 226 po. to two hiccorys on the Nuskarora Roade or path, thence along the Nuskarora Road or path until it meets with Nottaway Riv. at a small red oake & a beech tree by the foarding place Canatorah the strait line being N. 20 deg. E. 356 po., thence up along the S. side of Nottaway Riv. to the 1st place. The Land was due by trans of 28 persons, 24 Oct. 1701.

Mary Pepper	Rich. Griffeth	Alice Duglis
Wm. Oliver	John Saythen	Dan. ffisher
Robt. Clerke	Eliz. Oliver	Sam. Methen
Rich. Hobbs	Anne Storkes	Sarah Brothers
Eliz. Dobson	Jo. Magoone	Rich. Price
Tho. Roberts	David Strahan	Alice Pembic
John Abett	Thomas Smith	Jno. Sturges
Wm. Ogle	ffra. Pember	Hep. Bines
Tho. Knight	Margt. Davis	Corn. Akee
James Clay		

p. 395. Richard Gourd, 100 Acs., C. C. Co., N. side of Jones Hole nr. otherwise called Barlthorp Cr. & also the N. side of Nottaway Riv., beg. at a Spanish oake corner tree to Mr. Thomas Busby on the sd. Cr. run(n)ing thence along the sd. Busby Land N. 706 deg. E. 33 po. to a hiccory corner of the sd. Busby's Land, thence N. 47 deg. E. 33 po. to a red oake saplin to the sd. Busby's Land, thence East 7 deg. 1/4 & 1/8 S. 26 po. to a corner gum of the sd. Busby's Land near a greate live oak standing within the sd. Busby's Land, thence E. 71 deg.

396

and half S. 54 po. to the Nottaway path near a red oake sapplin thence W. 13 deg. 3/4 & 1/8 W. 40 po. to a white oake sapplin & red oake, thence S. 36 deg. W. 60 po. to a hiccory sapplin & a white oake, thence E. 41 deg. S. 43 po. to Solmonds Meadow Br., thence along Salmonds Meadow Br. run(n)ing out of the sd. Jones Hole (otherwise called Barkthorp Cr. - not closed) to a sapplin white oake, thence E. 72 deg. & 1/2 S. 56 po. to 2 Spanish oakes by 2 cross paths near a Woolfepitt, thence South 72 deg. & 1/2 W. 60 po. to a hollow butterwood and a papaw gum in a small Br. of the sd. Cr., thence up along the sd. Jones Hole alias Barlethorp Cr. to the beginning. The Land was due for 2 persons, 24 Oct. 1701, not named. At the foot of the Patent: Two rights paid for to Wm. Byrd, Esq., Auditor.

Bk. 9, p. 396. John Poythris, of Deep bottom, Sen'r., 350 Acs., on the N. side of Nottaway Riv. (the Patent does not say C. C. Co., but is is in the C. C. Co. index), beg. at an old dead oake by a Birch on the Riv. side & run(n)ing thence

along the tread line of a tract of 950 Acs., patented by
Hugh Lee & by him sold to Wm. Jones Sen'r., Robert Hix the
Taylor Sen'r & John Roberts, N. 1 deg. W. 96 po. to a white
oake in a fork of the Myery Br. that parts Conatora Old feild
& a small ash in the sd. Br., thence N. W. 120 po. to an heap
of marked trees on the top of an hill, thence S. 44 deg. W.
350 po. to an heap of marked trees on the Indian

397

Sw., thence down along the Indian Sw. & Nottaway Riv. to the
beginning. The Land was due for trans. of 7 persons, 24 Oct.
1701.

John Lee	Mary Drin	Heni Snetgrove
Robert Boreman	Humphry Hix	N. Standback
		Wm. Lambud

    p. 397. John ffreeman, 300 Acs., C. C.Co., on the S.
side of Nottaway Riv., beg. at a Pawpaw gum in Correhuesoe
Sw. & run(n)ing W. S. W. 14 po. to 2 red oakes thence N. W.
& by N. 102 po. to a gum and a hickory and a greathollow white
oake and a red splin, thence W. N. W. 96 po. to a white oake,
thence N. E. by N, 20 po., thence N. 11 deg. & 1/4 W. to a
Edloes Br. at a Pawpaw gum, thence down along the meadows
of Edloes Br. to the mouth of thereof, thence down along
Nottaway Riv. & the mouth of Corrohuessoe Sw., thence up along
the meadows of Correhuessoe Sw. on the N. side thereof to a
pine near the head of the sd. Sw., thence S. W. through the
head of the sd. Sw. to a Pawpaw gum with 2 "Body," thence down
the sd. Correhussoe Sw. to the beginning. The Land was due
for trans. of 6 persons, 24 Oct. 1701.
John ffreeman & Mary his wife & 4 rights paid for to
Wm. Byrd, Esq., Auditor.

    p. 398. William Jones, Sen'r., 600 Acs., C. C. Co.,
on both sides of Nottaway Riv., beg at the mouth of Jones
Hole & running thence up the same to a white oake and 2
hiccorys at the goeing over at the gum Logg, thence E. 53
deg. S. 45 po., thence E. 77 deg. & 1/2 S. 70 po. down into
the horse "pocoson," thence S. 14 deg. & 1/2 W. 112 po.
through the middle of the horse pocoson (or near it) to
Nottaway Riv., thence up along Nottaway Riv. according to
the meadnerings thereof on the N, side of the same, till it
comes opposite to the upward side of Edloes Br., thence
crossing the Riv. & so from the mouth of the sd. Edloes Br.
on the S. side of the Riv. W. 35 deg. and 1/8 N. 84 po. to
2 hiccory sapplins, thence W. 55 deg. N. 180 po. to a white
oak and 2 hiccorys on a point by a meadow by the lower tradeing
path, thence W. 5 deg. & 3/4 S. 120 po. to a red oak, thence S.
62 deg. W. 94 po. to a red oake and a white oake, thence W.
22 deg. N. 30 po. to a white oak a double bodyed, red oake
& hiccory between the edge of an Indian old feild and a
Sw., thence N. 7 deg. & 1/2 E. 60 po. to the sd. Nottaway Riv.
at three marked trees thence down the S. side of Nottaway
Riv., including all Islands on the S. side within the bounds
of this Land to the Mouth of Cone Hole, thence over the sd.
Nottaway Riv. to the beginning. The Land was due by trans.
of 12 persons, 24 Oct. 1701. John Rudds 4 times & 8 rights

more due by order of the Gen'l. Court held 21 Oct. 1699 to Robert Bolling & by him assigned as appears by the sd. order.

Bk. 9, p. 406. Thomas Wyn, 200 Acs., C. C. Co., S. side of Jones Hole Sw. & N. side of Nottaway Riv., beg. at a red oake on a point of an hill side by a Br. called Tradeing Br. in sight of the sd. Wyns Plantation & running thence S. 3 deg. E. 106 po. to a black oake by a Br. thence E. 36 deg. S. 275 po. to the line of Land of Hugh Lee Jun'r. now in possession of Wm. Jones Sen'r., Robert Hix Sen'r. & John Roberts, thence N. 45 deg. & 1/4 E. 87 po. & 1/2 to a hiccory corner tree to the sd. Lees Land by Cunatora path, thence W. 45 deg. & 3/4 N. 115 po. & to 3 White oakes and a black gum, thence W. 36 deg. N. 140 po., thence W. 23 deg. N. 106 po. to the beginning. The Land was due for trans. of 4 (not named) persons, 24 Oct. 1701. Note at the foot of the Patent: Four Rights paid for to Wm. Byrd, Esq., Auditor.

p. 407. John Buttler, 450 Acs., C. C. Co., Bristol Parish, N. side of Warrock Sw. next above the line of John Ledbeter, vizt., beg. at a corner white oake on the sd. Sw. & runs thence N. W. 50 po. to a pine, thence E. N. E. 34 po. to a corner white oake, thence N. N. W. 38 po. to a corner pine, thence W. N. W. 62 po. to a black oake, thence N. W. 42 po. to a corner black oake, thence N. 209 po. to a corner white oake, thence W. by N. 1/2 N.'ly 94 po. to a corner pine, thence N. W. by W. 96 po. to a corner pine, thence S. W. & by S. 88 po. to a corner pine, thence S. S. E. 140 po. to a corner white oake, thence W. S. W. 83 po. to a corner white oake, thence S. 58 po. to a corner black oake, thence S. by W. 80 po. to a corner black oake standing on Worrock Main Sw., thence down the sd. Sw. to the beginning. The Land was due for trans of 9 persons, 24 Oct. 1701.

Wm. Po-(as Ms.)	Robt. Tomson	John Burton
Tho. Whale	- Hudson	Jane Chapfeild
Eliza. Kidley	Robt. Ashley	John Moore

p. 420. Mr. Edmund Irby, 399 Acs., C. C. Co., (Note by the Editor: this Patent has been included among those for the S. side of the James River; Monkes Cr. has been taken to be the same as Monkey's Cr. This is subject to correction.) Both sides of white oake Sw., a Br. of Monkes Cr., beg. at the sd. Sw. on the Eastern side & run(n)ing thence E. 4 deg. N. 130 po. to a black oake by a Br. of the former Br., thence N. 4 deg. W. 200 po. to a greate pine by a main fork of the White Oak Sw., thence W. 4 deg. S. 104 po. crossing the sd. fork main Br. to an ash and an elm in the White Oake Sw., thence over the sd. White oake Sw. & up along the same to 2 red oakes on the sd. Sw., thence W. 4 deg. S. 195 po. to an heap of marked trees, thence S. 4 deg. E. 220 po. to a white oake and an hiccory saplins on the line of Mr. James Cock, thence E. 4 deg. N. 170 po. to the White Oake Sw. at the beginning. The Land was due by trans. of 8 persons, 24 Oct. 1701, not named. Note at the foot of the Patent: Eight Rights paid for to Wm. Byrd, Esq., Auditor.

p. 438. Lewis Greene, 203 Acs., C. C. Co., at the head of Wm. Ditties, which sd. W. D. bought of James Warradine, called high

Peake on the S. side of Baylys Cr. run(n)ing into the wood
S. by E. of Mr. John Georges Land 130 po. & E. by N. along
the woods 250 po. The Land was due: formerly granted to
James Paddon by Patent 10 March 1662, & deserted & to L. G.
by orders of the Gen'l. Court, 22 Oct. 1701 & for trans. of
4, not named, 25 Apr. 1702. Note at foot of the Patent:
four rights paid for to Wm. Byrd, Esq., Auditor.

    p. 451. James Williams, Charles W. & John W., sons of
John W., dec'd., 650 Acs., C. C. Co., Bristol Parish, vizt.,
beg. at a corner ash standing below ye mill on the S. side of
Gravely run & runs thence S. by W. 50 po. to a corner pohickory, thence W. 60 po. to a corner white oake, thence
N.N.W. 26 po. to a corner black oake, thence W. 300 po. to
a corner pine, thence S. 20 po. to a corner white oake, thence
W. 120 po. to a corner white oake, thence N. 126 po. to
a corner ash on Gravely run, thence up Gravely run as it
trends to a corner white oake, thence E. 46 deg. N. 180 po.
to a corner black oake, thence E. & by N. 100 po. cros(s)-
ing the 2nd. Br. to a corner pine, thence E. S. E., 224 po.
to a corner black oake standing on Mr. Jno. Herberts line,
thence on his line S. W. & by W. 17 po. to a corner butterwood standing on the N. side of Gravely run, thence down the
sd. run aa it trends to the beginning. The Land was due by
trans. of 13 persons, 25 April 1702.

Jacob Bapford	Richard Farmon	Rebecca George
Law: Bridges	Henry Knight	Jane Coby
John Whithall	Wm. Tuttle	Xto. Hill (All.)

(No County Index, for reference only. Bk. 9, p. 448, Richard
Holliman, on the S. side of the main Blackwater.)

(No County Index, probably belongs here, but subject to
correction. Bk. 9, p. 460, Capt. Harnison & Jno. Scot,
1700 Acs. on the S. side of the main Blackwater, beg. at a
poplar on the W. side of Acomorock Sw. & so runs N. 28 deg.
W. 58 po. to a White Oake, thence N. 3 deg. W. 88 po. to a
gum, thence N. 35 deg. W. 238 po. to a Hiccory in Tho: Cappels
& Ja: Jones his line thence up the sd. Cappells & Jones W.
12 deg. N. 267 cha. to a red oake, thence N. 35 deg. W. 143
po. to 2 small Hiccory saplins, thence N. 29 deg. W. 110 po.
to a Spanish oake thence W. 18 deg. N. 60 po. to a blacke
oake, thence S. 27 deg. W. 102 po. to a scrubby oake, thence
S. 36 deg. E. 320 po. to a white oake, thence S. 125 po. to
a hiccory, thence S. 25 deg.

E. 138 po. to a hiccory, thence E. 249 po. to a gum in a
small Br., thence S. 13 deg. E. 122 po. to a red Oake, thence
S. 28 deg. W. 127 po. to a scribby black oake, thence S. 20
deg. W. 154 po. to a red oake, thence S. 62 deg. E. 235 po.
to a Hiccory, thence S. 96 po. to a red oake, thence S. 37
deg. E. 80 po. to a Spanish oake, thence S. 150 po. to a
Hiccory, thence E. 84 po. to a hiccory, thence S. 16 deg. E.
51 po. to a red oake, thence S. 42 deg. W. 212 po. to a
hiccory, thence S. 102 po. to a black oake & a hiccory, thence
E. 4 deg. N. 104 po. to a white oake near the Acamorock Sw.,
thence along ye side of the sd. Sw. N. 5 deg. E. 240 po. to

a hiccory, thence N. 26 deg. W. 250 po. to a red oake thence N. 78 po. to a great pine, thence N. 33 deg. W. 208 po. to a live oake by ye side of a Br., thence N. 23 deg. W. 102 po. to a black oake, thence N. 50 deg. E. 196 po. to ye beginning. The sd. land was due by trans. of 34 persons, 25 April 1702.

Rich. Railey	Isabella Hodges	Elianor Taylor
Rich. Owen	Wm. Gilbert	John Walker
Eliza: Wood	John ffuller	Mary Page
Eliza: Richman	Anne Dickeson	Wm. Howard
Margt: Bourgh	Wm. Reynolds	Eliza. Duberly
John Williamson	Eliza: Sydenham	Sarah Daniel
Arnold Bradshaw	Wm. Davis	Mary Browne
Rachel Norman	John Brown	Mary Kees
Lydia Andrews	Mary Reede	Eliza: Wallis
Susanna Brown	Mary Drewe	Mary Smith
ffrancis Hill (All.)	Hester Vaughan	Wm. Southaway)

p. 403. James Salmon 376 Acs., S. side of Blackwater Sw., bounded: beg. at a hiccory on Jones hole Sw. & running thence S. 2 deg. E. 160 po. to a hiccory on ye sd. Sw., then down the sd. Sw. to a white oake into the woods, N. 34 deg. E. 72 po. to a pine, thence N. 29 deg. W. 116 po. to a white oake, thence W. 41 deg. N. 140 po. to a hiccory,

thence N. 17 1/2 deg. N. 68 po. to a Hiccory thence N. 12 deg. W. 116 po. to cross a Br. yt. makes out of the aforesd. Sw. to a chesnut oake, thence up the sd. Br. N. 6 1/2 deg. E. 164 po. to a black oake by the sd. Br., thence into the woods N. 42 deg. W. 50 po. to a red oake, thence W. 18 deg. S. 39 po. to a red oake, thence S. 47 1/2 po. to a white oake, thence E. 37 deg. S. 26 po. to a Hiccory by the Sw., thence down the sd. Sw. to the beginning. The sd. land was due by trans. of 8 persons, 28 Oct. 1702.

James Beddwick	Eliza: Corbin	And 2 rights more
John Curtis	Edward Freese	paid for to Wm. Byrd,
Wm. Edwards	John Barnes	Esq., Auditor.

p. 493. Robert Carlisle, a tract of 100 Acs. at a great pine near the line of Col. Wm. Randolph, Mr. ffrancis Epps & Mr. Robert Bolling on the N. side of the Warriches & running thence E. 47 deg. 1/2 & 1/3 S. 102 2/3po. to a path that goes from ye sd. Carlisles towards John Scotts at a red oake, black oake & a hiccory saplins on the sd. Randolphs, Epps & Bollings line, thence S. 87 4/6 deg. E. 36 po., thence over a Br. N. 83 deg. 1/2 & 1/8 E. 24 po. to the sd. Randolph, Epps & Bollings corner at a white oake by a Br. called the reedy Br., thence over the 1st. mentioned Br. being a Br. of the reedy Br. & along Thomas Cappells Land W. 7 deg. 3/4 & 1/3 N. 21 1/3 po. to a corner white oake of the sd. Cappells Land, thence ye same course 200 po. to a sapling white oake by a Br. comeing out of Unites Br., thence S. 37 1/8 deg. W. 140 po. to a pine & hiccory & red oake saplines, thence E. 47 deg. 1/4 & 1/3 S. 34 po. to the beginning. The sd. land was due by trans of 2 persons, not named, 28 Oct. 1702. At the foot of the Patent: 2 rights paid for to Wm. Byrd, Esq., Auditor. (Note of the Editor: this patent is listed in the C. C. Col. Index.)

(No County Index, Bk. 9, p. 519. William Williams, 400 Acres on the S. side of Blackwater Sw., beg. at a gum by the runs side of Holloway Sw. & so running S. 32 1/2 deg. W. 120 po. to a great pine, thence S. 27 deg. E. 78 po. to a pine thence S. 90 deg. E. 81 po. to a white oake, thence S. 31 deg. E. 270 po. to a white oake, thence S. 81 deg. E. 148 po. to a white oake at the mouth of a small Br. & stands by the runn side of the aforesd. Sw. & so up various courses of the run of the sd. Sw. to the beginning. The sd. land was due by trans. of 8 persons, not named, 24 April 1703. At the foot of the Patent: 8 rights paid for to Wm. Byrd, Esq., Auditor.)

(No County, Bk. 9, p. 523, Thomas Senior, for reference only. It is upon the heads of ye main Branches of Upper Chippokes Cr., formerly to Tho. Senior, 6 Apr. 1664. For the Patent of 6 April 1664, see Bk. 5, 368 (402).

p. 524. William Temple, 627 Acs., C. C. Co., on the S. side of Ja: Riv. on Warewick Sw., vizt., beg. at 2 white oakes on the N. side of the above sd. Sw., thence N. 44 deg. W. 120 po. along John Ledbiters Line to a corner red oake, thence E. 9 deg. - 238 po. to a pine, thence E. 40 deg. S. 51 1/2 po. to a pine, thence E. 11 1/2 deg. 82 po. to a shrubb oake, thence S. 40 deg. E. 44 1/2 po. to a red oake, thence S. 14 deg. E. 42 po. to a Spanish oake, thence

525

S. 23 deg. E. 90 po. to a white oake, thence S. 17 deg. W. 60 po. to a white oake on ye S. side of the above sd. Sw., thence W. 20 deg. N. 61 po. to a white oake W. 11 deg. N. 98 po. to a shrubb white oak thence W. 41 1/2 deg. N. 44 po. to a pine, thence W. 11 deg. S. 58 po. to a pine, thence W. 41 deg. N. 82 po. to a shrubb oake, thence S. 22 deg. W. 72 po. to a white oake, thence W. 10 deg. N. 320 po. to a red oake & hiccory, thence N. 37 1/2 deg. E. 66 po. to a red oake, thence N. 44 po. to a gum on the S. side of the main water course of the above sd. Warwick Sw., thence down the same to 2 white oakes where it began. The sd. land was due by trans. of 13 persons, 24 April 1703 (see next page.)

Mary Davis	Henry Morgan	Robert Kellett
Duke Davis	John Ray	Antho: Hales
Tho: Ashley	Edward Bayly	Wm. Harris
Anne Bridges	Jon: Badd	Charles Colliford
	John Right	

p. 571. Robert Bolling, 365 Acs., Bristol Parish, C. C. Co., beg. at a black oake, side line to sd. Overlies Land (Note of Editor: there is no earlier mention of Overly), being a tract of 323 Acs. formerly taken up & Patented by sd. Overley, the sd. line being a W. 27 d. S. line 89 po. & running thence S. 15 deg. W. 104 po. to a pine by a slash called the Round Pond, thence S. 50 deg. W. 60 po. to the Western Trading Path at a red oake near the upper side thereof, thence S. 24 deg. W. 166 po. to 2 black oakes & a pine at the head of a Br. on a point thence N. 64 deg. W. 109 po. to Ralph Jackson's line at a small red oake, thence along the sd. Jacksons Land, thence along sd. Jackson Line W. 32 deg. 1/2 N. 72 po. to a white oake corner of the sd.

Jacksons Land, N. 1 deg. W. 44 po. to the sd.Jacksons corner thence N. 23 deg. E. 120 po. to a verubed black oake, thence N. 104 po. to a gum in a Br. of Rohoick in the line of Mr. Rich. Jones, thence along the sd. Jones line E. 1 1/4 deg. N. 82 po. to the sd. Jones's corner at 2 saplin red oake & a pine by the head of a Br. of Rohoick, thence along the sd. Jones line N. 10 3/4 deg. E. 65 po. to an Hiccory corner tree to the sd. Jones & Henry Walls land N. 29 3/4 deg. E. 17 po. to a small red oake corner of ye sd. Walls at or near the main Br. of Rohoick on a hillside, thence along the sd. Walls Land E. 13 3/4 deg. N. 13 po. to the main Br. of Rohoick, thence up the main Br. of Rohoick along the sd. Overbyes (as in the Ms.) old Land S. by E. 116 po. to a pine, thence along the sd. Overbyes Land E. 27 deg. N. 96 po. to the beginning. The sd. land was formerly granted to Nich. Overby by Patent, 26 Apr. 1698, deserted & since to R. B. by order of the Gen'l. Court, 22 April 1703, further granted & by trans. of 8 persons, not named, 23 Oct. 1703. At the foot of the Patent: 8 rights paid for to Wm. Byrd, Esq., Auditor.

p. 571. John Poythress, an irregular tract of 609 Acs., C. C. Co., in the Black water, on the S. side of Ja: Riv. & S. side of Blackwater, at a pine & running thence S. S. W. 30 Cha. to a corner

thence S. E. by S. 40 cha. to a corner black oake, thence E. 31 cha., thence S. E. 61 cha. to ye Nottaway Path continued 18 cha. to the 1st. Br. 102 cha. to the 2nd Br. continued 33 cha. to the Blackwater Spring contained 31 cha. to a corner pohicey, thence S. E. by E. 12 cha., thence E. by N. 12 cha. to the 3rd. Br. continued 88 cha. to the Blackwater Maine Sw. to a beech marked 4 ways, thence bounding N. along the Sw. near the line of Capt. Robert Wyes 13 cha. & N. E. 13 cha. & N. E. by N. 11 cha. & N. E. by E. 34 cha. & N. E. 22 cha. & E. 5 cha. & N. E. by E. 20 cha. & N: N. E. 16 cha. as the Sw. winds to a reedy Br. to a white oake marked 4 ways, thence N. 46 cha. to a corner black oake, thence W. S. W. 16 cha. to a great Sw., thence continued over the great Sw. 16 cha. to a pine marked 4 ways, thence S. W. by W. 20 cha., thence W. 62 cha. to the Br. that comes by Fownes his quarter continued 40 cha. to a white oake marked 4 ways, thence W. N. W. 39 cha. to the line of Hercules fflood, thence for 50 Acs. he bought of the sd. fflood S. W. 40 cha. to a meadow taking in a point of Land continuing 50 cha., thence up the main Sw. W. & W. by S. & W. S. W. 200 Cha. to the beginning. The sd. land was formerly granted to ffrancis Poythress & by Patent, 28 Sept. 1681 & deserted & to sd. John P. by order of Gen'l. Court, 21 April 1703, and further due by trans. of 13 persons, 23 Oct. 1703 (for those trans., see next page.)

Robt. Lloyd   Eliz. Brumfeild   Paid me, Auditor
Rich. Wilkinson   Charles Bartholemew   Bird, for 6 rights.
Joyce Bibiell   Patrick Counoley
                      Eliz. Smith

p. 582. Benj. ffoster, 223 Acs., C. C. Co., S. side of Blackwater, at the mouth of Georges Meadow & so up the water course of the same to a red oake in Mr. James Minge's line in the fork of the above sd. meadow at or near the head thereof & from above sd. oake in Minges Line W. 30 deg. N. 37 cha. to a corner pine, thence N. 17 deg. W. 25 1/2 cha. to a red oake, thence N. 40 1/2 deg. W. 22 1/2 cha. to a white shrubb oake, thence W. 16 1/2 N. 48 1/2 cha. to a red oake, thence N. 41 deg. W. 39 cha. to a corner hiccory upon the maine Warwick road from Welches to Busby's & from the above sd. Hiccory N. 47 deg. E. 53 cha. to the main course of the Blackwater, thence down the same to the mouth of George's meadow where it began. The sd. land was due by trans. of 5 persons, not named, 23 Oct. 1703. At the foot of the Patent: Paid Wm. Byrd, Esq., for 5 rights.

    p. 656. John Hamlyn, 550 Acs., C. C. Co., Westopher Parish & on the S. side of the James Riv., beg. at a line of Dan. Higdon & runs thence along his line S. 164 po. to a corner Spanish oake, thence S. E. 132 po. to a corner Spanish oake, thence E. 148 po. to a corner pine, thence S. 220 po. to a corner black oake on the line of Wm. Edmunds & John Williams, thence along their line W. S. W. 54 po. to a corner pine, thence N. N. W. 90 po. to a corner pine, thence W. by N. 156 po. to a corner black oake, thence N. W. & by N. 290 po. along Edmunds line to a corner black oake, thence on Mr. Bates his line N. N. E. 32 po. & N N. W. 180 po. to a corner white oake on the Line of Maj. Poytheress, thence along his lines E. S. E. 148 po. to a corner black oake, thence E. 76 po. to the beginning. The sd. land was formerly granted to Charles Goodrich by Patent dated 20 Apr. 1687 & deserted & since to J. H. & further due by trans. of 11 persons, 2 May 1705.

Robert Blight	Tho. Lewis	Paid Wm. Bird
John Unit	Eliz: Jenings twice	for 5 rights.
	Roy Taylor	

The end of the abstracts of the Patents of Charles City County.

THE PRINCE GEORGE COUNTY LAND PATENTS

Book 9

p. 663. Land in Pr. Geo. Co., 300 Acs., late in possession of Matthew Yates, dec'd., lately escheated, Inquisition under Wm. Randolph, Gent., Escheater of the sd. Co., Jury 13 Jan. 1703 & Benjamin Evans of Pr. Geo. Co., has made his composition & so granted, 2 May 1705.

p. 676. Adam Heath, 681 Acs., Pr. Geo. Co., & Surry Co., bounded: beg. at a live oake sapling by an old tree that is falne by the side of the Western run of upper Chippoax & run(n)ing, thence W. 40 deg. N. 144 po. to a Hiccory corner of Burcher land, thence N. 4 1/2 deg. E. 82 po. to Wm. Salvages line by the Quagmire Br. near a pine in the sd. Salvages line & a white oake corner tree of this land, thence along the sd. Salvages N. 39 2/3 deg. W. 144 po. to a pine corner tree of sd. Salvage, thence W. 10 deg. N. 100 po. to a black gum in a Br. of that Quagmire, thence S. 36 deg. W. 35 po. to a pine, thence S. 58 1/4 deg. W. 76 po. to 2 scrubbed black oakes, thence S. 35 deg. W. 88 po. to a white oake by low ground, thence W. 6 deg. 3/4 & 1/2 1/4 N. along a slash or Br. 50 po. to Crochsons line at a sapling oake, thence S. 32 1/3 deg. W. 19 po. to a corner pine of the line at a sapling oake, thence S. 32 1/3 deg. W. 19 po. to a corner pine of the sd. Crochsons, thence along Crockson watling & marhes Lands S. 66 1/4 deg. W. 212 po. to a red oake by a small slash or Br., thence S. 45 deg. W. 96 po. to a white oake, thence S. 51 deg. E. 69 1/2 po. to a red oake thence N. 6 deg. 3/4 & 1/2 1/4 E. 10 po. to a corner pine of the land of Abraham Heath dec'd., thence along of Abraham Heath dec'd. E. 28 deg. 1/4 & 1/2 S. 51 po. to a pine in the line of Abraham Heath dec'd. being a corner tree of Adam Heath's land, thence along the land of Adam Heath N. 54 1/4 deg. E. 24 po. to a black oake corner tree of the sd. Heath, thence along the sd. Heaths land W. 31 1/4 & 1/2 deg. N. 20 1/2 po. to a pine by the round pinq slash; thence along the land of John Wapple now in possession of the sd. Adam Heath N. 55 ¼ ¼ ¼ deg. E. 197 1/2 po. to a white oake 6 po. from a corner pine of the sd. Wapples on an E. 41 ½ ¼ deg. S. Course, thence along the sd. Wapples land E.

677

4 ½ deg. S. 204 po. to a corner tree, thence S. 176 po. over the Western run of upper Chippoakes, up a small Br. of the same along Barrow ye sd. old Road that goes to Wm. Shorts at a corner red oake 176 po. thence by the sd. path to a red oake near the sd. path, thence W. 50 3/4 deg. N 42 po. to a white oake, thence W. 65 3/4 deg. N. 12 po. to the beginning. The sd. land was formerly granted to sd. Adam Heath by Patent, 563 acs., the residue being waste land is due to him for trans. of 12 persons, 2 May 1705.

Jane Tompson	Margaret Tompson	Mary Tompson
Wm. Tompson	Mary Tompson	Eliz. Tompson
Dan. Room	Abraham Wahire	Edw. Raclift
Annis Jaines	Mary Jones	Peter Pavile

p. 705. Lewis Greene, 97 Acs., Pr. Geo. Co., Viz., beg. at a maple on the S. side of Jones hole, thence along the lines of William Jones Sen'r. N. 24 deg. W. 102 po. to a maple in a Br., thence W. 13 ½ deg. N. 104 ½ po. to a white shrubb oake, thence W. 23 deg. S. 71 ½ po. to a hickory being the corner of Mr. Tho. Wynn, thence down the same Jones hole, thence down the same according to the several meanders thereof to the beginning. The sd. land was due by trans. of 2 persons, 2 Nov. 1705.
Sam. Burefoy   Thomas Hooper

(p. 706. Benjamin Harrison, Gent., 220 Acs., (No County index,) on the S. side of Nottaway Riv., beg. at a white oake, thence S. 34 deg. W. 400 po. to 2 red oakes (of) Capt. Hunts corner trees, thence along the sd. Hunts line S. 2 deg. E. 72 po. to a red oake, another of sd. Hunts corner trees, thence along another of the sd. Hunts lines, E. 22 deg. S. 36 po. to a red oake in a corner tree of the sd. Hunts, then S. 28 po. to a Hickory, thence 4 deg. S. 46 po. to an old dead red oake, the W. 16 ½ deg. N. 70 po. to a Hiccory, thence N. 19 deg. E. 96 po. to a white oake, then N. 38 ½ deg. W. 180 po. to a red oak, then N. 10 deg. E. 142 po. to a red oake, then N. 35 deg. W. 130 po. to a hiccory, then N. 25 deg. W. 36 po. to a pine, then E. 30 deg. N. 50 po. to a hiccory, then N. 18 ½ deg. W. 130 po. to a white oake on the E. side of a Reedy Br., then down the sd. Br. to a white oake standing in the mouth of the sd. Br., then E. 22 ½ deg. N. 144 po. to a hiccory on the Nottaway Riv., thence down the sd. Riv. to the beginning. The sd. land was due for imp. of 44 persons, 2 Nov. 1705.

John Wilkins	John Laugher	Elinor Hunt
James Russell	George Jackson	Mary Oliver
Thomas Pyder	Arthur Kenselaugh	Edward Kelley
Lawr. Ball	John Roach	Alice White
John Walker	Thomas Roch	Kath: Kenton
Turler Meison	Dennis Rooark	Mary Lane
Thomas Jackson	Patrick Earne	Mary Wheeler
Robert Harrison	James Theary	Robert Reeves
James Stanley	Anthony Dencely	Thomas fflattman
John ffloyd	John Connell	Charles Moorehead
ffrancis Wheeler	John Poove	Thomas Price
Kath. ffling	Anthony Bateman	Margaret Bryan
Mary Lilly	Issabella Davis	Jane Shirly
2 rights to Mr. Auditor	Rich. Booth	John Poore)

p. 711. Richard Bland, 254 Acs., Pr. Geo. Co., upon Blackwater on the E. side of the Reedy Br., having the land of Wm: Harris & Adam Tapley for bounds thereof on the E. side (of) the lands of Capt. Henry Batts & the main woods on the S. side (of) the main woods & the Reedy Br. & the lands of Mr. ffrancis Poythress on the N. side begin(n)ing at a heap of marked pines standing in the long meadow w:ch joynes upon Ealeroot Levell & run(n)ing S. 2/3 of a deg. W. 108 po. to a corner tree of ye sd, land of Wm. Harris & Adam Tapley, thence along a line of the sd. Harris & Tapley S. 2 deg. E. 164 po. to a red oake, thence along another line of Harris & Tapley S. 30 deg. W. & beyond the sd. lines of the sd. Harris & Tapley to the 2nd Sw. the same course 108 po., thence along ye 2nd Sw. W. 9 deg. N. 24 po. to a black oake the side of a knowle, thence N. 18 deg. W. 44 po. to a corner tree of Capt. Henry Batts land, being a great white oake & till the same course to another corner of the sd. Batts land, being a black oake 22 po. more, thence 40 deg. W. 42 po. to a black oake, thence N. 72 deg. W. 330 po. to a great marked pine, thence N. 13 deg. W. 280 po. to the further side of Reedy Br. to a young pine comprehending all the sd. Reedy Br., within the sd. bounds, thence to the meanders of ye Reedy Br. N. 57 1/2 deg. E. 387 po. to Maj. ffrancis Poythress his land, thence along the sd. Poythress his land to a corner thereof, being a red oake S. 23 deg. W. 60 po., thence along the sd. Poythress land S. 31 ½ deg. E. 25 po. (to) another corner tree, being a pine, thence along sd. Poythress land 32 deg. E. 154 po. to a black oake, thence S. 46 deg. E. 138 po. to the beginning. The sd. land was formerly granted by Patent, 21 Apr. 1690 to Hercules fflood, deserted & since to R. B. by order of the Gen'l. Council, 20 Apr. 1705 & further due by imp. of 25 persons, 2 Nov. 1705 (Imp. on next page).

John Deom	Wm. Cooke	Robt. Ireland
Edw. Bowman	Jane Hatchman	John Reeding
Robt. Crowther	ffran. Cook	Anne Parkes
John Pourour	Wm. Aldus	Dorothy Reach
Rich. Dunn	Tho: Loyd	Henry May
ffra. Aldus	Sam. Temple	Walte Higgins
Alex. O Hern	Tho: Plowman	Sam. Olden
Tho: Douse	Tho: Howlett	Tho: Pluckrose
John Battice	Tho: Straing	(Acreage?)

p. 714. Robert Bolling, Col., 1973 Acs., Pr. Geo. Co., bounded: beg at the mouth of Monosonsek Cr., thence up the same to the Cross Br., thence along the same to Stony Cr. to Nottaway Riv., thence down Nottaway Riv., to the several meanders to ye mouth of Monosoneck (to) the beginning. The sd. land was for trans. of 40 persons, 1 May 1706.

Geo: Benford	Matt. Deane	Mary Ponyard
Matt: Eennys	Wm. Jemson	John ffox
Cha: Windham	Geo: Easleton	Anne ffuring
Tho: York	Nicho: Arnold	Tho: Burton
Theo: Peirson	Anne Armstead	John Hardiman
Joan Woodward	Sam. Thurwell	Rich. Lookman
Margt. Nicholes	Tho: Brown	James Walke
Debora Mumford	Rich. Merchant	Eliza: Putman
Isabell Collyer	Peter Russell	Hannah Selby
Eliza. fflorence	Geo. Homes	Sarah Clerk
Tho: Hanford	John Boss	John Butler
Sarah Cooper	Wm. Wilkeson	Tho: Jones
Ed: Benn	Wm. England	Mary Ball
Mary James	(Acreage?)	

p. 714. Robert Mumford, 351 Acs., Pr. Geo. Co., in Monosoneck Cr., bounded: beg. at a corner tree of Mutus Butler on the side of Rowanty Sw., thence along the sd. Butlers line N. 38 ½ deg. E. 100 po. to a white oake & poplar, thence S. 12 deg. E. 120 po a pine, thence S. 54 po. to a red oake, thence S. 42 deg. W. 56 po. to a sweet gum, thence 10 deg. E. 86 po. to a white oake, thence S. 41 deg. E. (left blank) - 4 po., thence S. 25 deg. E. 65 ½ po. to a white oake, thence N. 29 deg. E. 36 ½ po. to a red oake, thence E. 40 deg. S. 36 po. to a pine thence S. 15 deg. W. 82 ½ po to a pine, thence S. 26 ½ deg. W. 66 po. to a hiccory, thence S. 3 ½ deg. W. 49 po. to a shrubb white oake, thence S. 43 ½ (deg.) W. 34 po. to a white oake, thence W. 5 deg. N. 24 po. to Monosoneck Cr., thence up the same & Rowanty Sw. to the beginning. The sd. land was for trans. of 7 persons, 1 May 1706.

Hannah Barker   Thomas Smart   John Decus
Mary Selistile   Rich. Morris   Eliza. Surgill
                Margt. Brook

p. 715. Mr. John Anderson & Mr. Robt. Mumford, 405 Acs., Pr. Geo. Co., bounded: beg. near the line of Henry King on the S. side of Noccosoneck Cr., thence S. 5 deg. W. 61 po. to a hiccory W. 27 deg. S. 27 ½ po. to a pine thence S. 5 deg. W. 228 po. to a red oake, thence E. 16 deg. S. 127 po. to a red oake, thence S. 40 deg. E 50 ½ po. to a corner pine, thence S. 10 ½ deg. E. 111 ½ po. to a pine, thence W. 40 deg. S. 88 po. to a red Br., thence down the sd. Br. 120 po., thence N. 14 ½ (deg.) W. 88 ½ po. to a hiccory, thence N. 45 deg. E. 42 ½ po. to a white oake, thence W. 17 deg. N. 63 ½ po. to a red oake, thence W. 44 deg. N. 47 ½ po. to a white shrubb oake, thence N. 16 deg. E. 76 po., thence W. 26 ½ (deg.) N. 48 po. to a red oake, thence N. 39 deg. W. 58 po.

to a white oake, thence E. 21 deg. N. 45 po. to a red oake, thence N. 5 deg. W. 24 ½ po. to a white oake, thence W. 32 deg. N. 104 ½ po. to a shrubb white oake, thence N. 11 ¼ (deg.) 125 po., to a corner, thence W. 19 ½ deg. N. 34 ½ po. to the beginning. The sd. land was due for trans. of 8 persons 1 May 1706.

James King   Hannah Hodkins   Cha: Ogleby
John Lewis   Daniell Harley   Tho: Yeoman
Timo: Bonus   John Hall

p. 718. Mr. Richard Bland, 16 Acs., Pr. Geo. Co., bounded beg. at a corner Spanish oake of Mr. Robert Mumford along his Line S. 11 ¼ deg. W. 46 po. to the dry Bottom Water course to an ash, thence E. 31 deg. 17 po. along Capt. Stiths Line, thence N. 35 deg. E. 32 po., thence N. 15 deg. E. 23 po., thence N. 23 deg. E. 26 po., thence N. 7 deg. (-?) 24 po. to Bicors Cr., thence up the same to a gum on the side of ye same thence S. 22 ½ deg. E. 26 po. to the beginning. The sd. land was due by trans. of 1, 1 May 1706. James Greeson.

p. 718. Mr. Richard Bland, 43 Acs., Pr. Geo. Co., bounded beg. at the corner of Mr. Robt. Mumfords Land, thence along his Lines N. 22 ½ deg. W. 26 po. to a gum on the side of Bicors Cr. or run, thence W. 22 (½ deg.) S. 256 po. to a stump in the Line of Mr. John Woodlife, thence along the sd. Woodlifs Line N. 33 po. to an ash on the side of Bicors Run, thence upon Wm. Mayes his land E. 10 deg. N. 26 po., thence E. 25 ½ po., thence E. 6 ½ (deg.) S. 46 ½ po, thence E. 19 ½ deg. S. 31 ½ po. intersecting the 2nd. course att a

sicamore, the corner of Mr. John Hardimann. The sd. land was due for trans. of 1 persons, 1 May 1706.
John Withers

p. 740. Benja: Harrison, Jr., Gent., 4583 Acs., Pr. Geo. Co., on both sides of Nottaway River, beg. at a hiccory on the banck of the N. side of Nottaway Riv. against a barr of Rocks, thence W. 8 3/4 deg. N. 38 po. to 2 small hiccorys S. 11 ½ deg. 27 po. to a pine thence S. 29 deg. 36 po. to a gum, thence S. 20 deg. E. 45 po. to a pine, thence W. 6 deg. N. 42 po. to a hiccory, thence W. 7 deg. & ½ S. 16 po. to a shrubb white oake, thence W. 38 deg. S. 35.

741

po to a hiccory, thence W. 8 deg. N. 58 po. to a shrubb white oake, thence W. 24 deg. S. 62 po. to (a) pine Crossing Harry Sw. at 20 po., thence S. 31 deg. W. 120 po. to a red oak, thence W. 25 ¼ deg. S. 118 po. to a red oake, thence S. 21 ½ deg. W. 93 po. to a meadow called Dukes Cooler, thence up the same to a pine, thence W. 16 deg. S. 80 po. to a pine, thence W. 65 po. to a pine, thence W. 29 deg. N. 173 po. to a shrubbe white oake, thence N. 11 deg. E. 44 po. to a red oake, thence W. 26 deg. N. 9. po. to a hiccory, thence W. 8 deg. N. 76 po. to a red oake, thence W. 38 deg. N. 40 po. to a red oake, thence W. 35 deg. N. 426 po. to a Spanish oake, thence W. 204 po. to a corner shrubb white eake, thence N. 45 deg. W. 150 po. to a white oake, thence E. 41 deg. N. 90 po. to a red oake, thence W. 427 po. to 2 red oakes, thence N. W. 102 po. to Will. Jones's Br., thence down the sd. Br. to Nottaway Riv., thence down the Nottaway Riv. to the mouth of a Br. on the S. side of Nottaway Riv. which falls into the Riv. against the Great Island, thence up that sd. Br. to a white oake thence E. 22 deg. S. 454 po. to an ash in the Spring Br., thence E. 9 deg. N. 148 po. to a hiccory N. 29 ½ deg. E. 189 po. to a red oake, thence E. 10 deg. N. 89 po. to a hiccory, thence E. 35 deg. S. 208 ½ po. to a red oake, thence E. 20 deg. S. 105 po. to a shrubb white oake, thence E. 10 deg. S. 174 po. to a hiccory,, thence N. 33 deg. E. 20 po. to a red oak, thence E. 32 ½ deg. S. 50 po. to a red oake, thence E. 15 deg. N. 146 po. to a shrubb oake, thence 8 ½ deg. S. 66 po. to a pine, thence E. 27 deg. N. 63 po. to a pine, thence N. 4 deg. W. 20 po. to a red oak, thence E. 6 deg. N. 26 po. to a pine by the side of a slash, thence N. 40 deg. E. 40 po. to a white oake, thence E. 31 deg. S. 31 po. to a gum, thence E. 27 ½ deg. N. 34 po. to a gum, thence N. 15 deg. (-?) po. to a red oake, thence E. 36 deg. N. 46 po. to a live oake, thence N. 12 deg. W. 37 po. to a red oake at the head of a Br. of Chetockcaurah Cr. or Sw., thence down the sd. Br. to Cheteheaurah Cr. or Sw., thence down the same to Nottoway.

742

Riv., thence down Nottoway Riv. to the beginning. The sd. land was due for the trans. of 92 persons, 10 June 1706.

David Kerne	Hugh Macdannell	Elline Phillips
James Loope	Oweb Boyle	Patrick Annimer
Law: Ferne	Geo: Baykervyle	Sam. Mitchell

Margt. Morris	Henry Hambrok	Sampson Gayer
Margt. Hand	Honor Weles	Wm. James
Patrick Nayor	Tho: Reale	Jer. Grantham
Teague Kelly	Tho. Lolly	Lawrence Trea
Margt. Mullins	Wm. Liddon	Teague King
Jno. Mc:Lanna	Tho. Corne	Michael Kelly
Roger Dreg	Susannah Palmers	Tho. Burke
Sarah Carty	John Gaines	Ellinor Carmon
Sam. Short	Toby Kelly	Ellinor Morris
Geo. Newton	Anne Meack	Ellinor Helbert
Wm. Kalleron	Patrick Hatfield	Edm. Kennold
Tho: Radish	Alice Mealey	Eliza. Pattin
Nora Higgens	Edw. Butler	(All.)

And 45 rights more paid for to Mr. Auditor Byrd.
Signed E. E. Thacker.

Book 10

p. 40. John Sadler, Citizen & Grocer of London & the Rev. Joseph Richardson, Clerk, husband of Ellinor Richardson, Ex'x of Thomas Quincy, late of London, Brewer, one of the certain tract or parcel of Land 2208 Acs., in the Parish of - (the blank is in the Ms.), Pr. Geo. Co., called Merchants Hope, & bounded: at an elm on the bank of Jas. Riv. --- to Powells Cr. -- to Jas. Riv. --- to the beginning. The sd. land was due to the sd. Sadler & Richardson by several purchases, 358 Acs. being surplus, 28 Apr. 1711 & for the trans. of 8 persons

James Naughty	Honore Shelone	Lydia Armefield
Katherine Jones	Susanna Redwood	Sarah Jones
Susanna Woodbridge	James fflanagin	

p. 40. to same, Tract of Land called Martin Brandon, 5037 Acs. of High ground, Sw. & Marsh, Pr. Geo. Co., bounded: at the mouth of Hackery Cr. --- to a gut by the side of a Br. or Slash, thence up the same --- to a hickory on the Bank of the Jas. Riv. at a place called the Church Landing, then down the Jas. Riv. by the meandering of it, including Tappahannah Marsh, to the mouth of Chipokes Cr., up it --- to the beginning. Which Tract was formerly granted to Simon Turges & Richard Quincy of London, merchants, Patent 5 Aug. 1643 for 4550 Acs., being due to them from the heirs of Capt. John Martin, late of Va., dec'd.: 4050 Acs., of the sd. land were by order of the Grand Assembly in March 1643 & 500 Acs., the residue by Capt. John Martin, 9 June 1643, being formerly given as a Glebe to the pish. of Martin Brandon & 487 Acres being surplus, 28 Apr. 1711 & trans. of:

Joseph Parish	Richard Cross	Elizabeth Wool
Ann Tool	Jos. Taylor	Henry Brimble

p. 51. Charles Williams, of the Co. of (the space is in the Ms.; it must have been considered by the person who indexed these Patents as of Pr. Geo. Co.) a tract of 347 Acs., in the Pish. of (the space is in the Ms.) in the Co. of Pr. Geo. on the S. side of Blackwater Sw., bounded: at a corner pine of John Butler, on the Cabbin Br., thence along his line --- to the Hogpen Br., thence up the same to good gainer Corner pine & thence along his line --- cross the Hogpen

Br., thence --- to an ash in the upper ffork of Little Hell or Stricts (this word may be Hicks or Hicts) Br., thence down the same to John Butler's line & along the line --- to the beginning, 19 Dec. 1711 & for trans of

Thomas Lewes	Robert Peale	John Brown
Jane Ely	Eliza: Eaton	Priscilla Harvey
	Eliza: Spencer	

    p. 51. William Rives, of Co. of - (the space; is in the Index of Pr. Geo. Co.,) Tract of 422 Acs. in Pish of - (space in Ms.) in the Co. of Pr. Geo. Co. and on Blackwater Sw., bounded: at a corner white oake of John Butler on the E. side of flinities Br., thence along Butler's line --- to the main water course of Blackwater Sw., thence down the same --- to Benja: ffosters line --- to Unities Br., thence down the same to the beginning, 19 Dec. 1711 & trans. of:

Thomas Potts	Richard fflahaven	John Brocke
Edward Ladde	Mary Coebb	

    p. 52. Thomas Parrum, of the Co. of - (space in Ms.; in Pr. Geo. Co. Index,) a tract of 153 Acs., in the Pish of - (space in Ms.), Co. of Pr. Geo., on both sides of Moccosonich (?) Cr., bounded: at a corner shrub white oake of George Tillman on the N. side of the sd. Cr., thence along his line S. --- to a pine in a small Br. of Cattayle Meadow, thence up along the side of the same --- to the beginning, 19 Dec. 1711; there is no ref. to trans. & no list of names.

    p. 66. Bisard Goodrich (in the margin and the Index and in the text the name is given as Edward Goodrich, except in the title,) Inq., Pr. Geo. Co., 12 Oct., 9th year of our reign, 100 Acs., escheated, Wm. Randolph, our Escheator, in Pr. Geo. Co., from Richard Dodd, granted now to Bisard Goodrich, 16 Apr. 1712.

    p. 77. Wm. Stainbank (the margin & text are difficult to read; the Index has Stainback,) of the Co. of (space in the Ms., but it is Index lists it as of Pr. Geo. Co.,) a Tract of 200 Acs., pish. of - (space in Ms.) of Pr. Geo., bounded: at a Butterwood on the Inter course of the Great Br. of James Hole Sw., thence --- to Wm. Raines Line, thence along the same to the Inter course of the Great Br. of James Hole Sw., thence up the Sw. --- to the beginning, 2 May 1713 & trans. of

John Reece	John Jackson	Alex. Sutton
	Tho. Bennet	

    p. 125. Inq., C. C. Co., 4 March 1702, before Wm. Randolph, Escheator for C. C. Co., now Pr. Geo. Co., a parcel of Land in Pr. Geo. Co. near Merchants Hope, upon the poplar level, which was called Robert Jones level; escheated from John Banister, late of sd. C. C. Co., now granted to James Binford; bounded: at a white oak in the fork of the Cross Br. & upon the Sw., thence up the Cross Br. --- in Warradine's line --- on the water course of poplar Sw., 16 June 1714.

    p. 144. John Scott, of Pr. Geo. Co., a tract of land of 221 Acs., on the S. side of Warrick Sw., Pr. Geo. Co., adj. his own land & bounded: at Epes corner white oak in his own line, thence along his own line --- to Epes line, thence along

the same --- to the beginning, 16 June 1714. (The Patent was)
For the consideration of 5 s. to the Gov'r. (No trans. are
named.)

  p. 144. Thomas Anderson, 105 Acs., Pr. Geo. Co., bounded:
on the Catatail in Kibbey Br. --- 16 June 1714. (The Patent
was for) Consideration of 10 s.

  p. 178. John Nickells, whereas 7 April 1694, there was
granted to Thomas Chappel 423 Acs., in C. C. Co., on the S.
side of Jas. Riv., now Pr. Geo. Co., on the Otterdam Sw.,
being the corner of the sd. Sw., being the corner of the land
of Tho. Smith & running on his line --- crossing a Great Br.
thence up the Br. --- crossing the Otterdam Sw. --- to the line
of Tho: Blunt('s) house on Blunt's line --- to the Otterdam
Sw., which tract was granted on consideration of seating &
the sd. Chappell failed to seat it & it was granted to John
Nickolls, 16 June 1714

  p. 197. Robert Rives, a tract of 219 Acs. in Pr. Geo.
Co. on the S. side of Nottoway Riv., bounded: at a corner
red oak of Wm. Jones, Sen'r. on the bank of the Riv., thence
along his line, ---, 16 Dec. 1714 & trans. of:

Wm. Singleton	Chas. Tannard	Wm. Steward
Wm. Greeson	John Hopkins	

  p. 198. Richard Hudson, a tract of 401 Acs. in Pr. Geo.
Co., bounded: at a corner dividing (of) sd. Hudson & Wm.
Maise, thence --- to a Butterwood on the Water course of
Hatchen's Run ---, 7 Dec. 1714. The land was due for trans.
of:

John Prichard	Tho. Scarlett	Joseph Smith
Wm. Hanks	John Hatfield	Tho. Sessions
James Morris	Anne Able	

  p. 198. William Maise, 401 Acs., in Pr. Geo. Co., bounded
at a Br. on the side of Hutchens Run, thence --- a corner white
oake of John Bannister, thence along Bannister's land --- to
a corner white oak, being the corner between the sd. Maise &
Richard Hudson ---, 16 Dec. 1714. The sd. land was for trans.
of:)

John Massey	Anne Massey	Matthew Row
Thomas Hughlett	Nath Kodgeson	Robt. Wilskins
James Cowherd	Wm. Kilsony	

  p. 198. John Nicholls, Gent., 217 Acs., on the S. side
of Blackwater Sw. in Pr. Geo. Co., bounded: at a white oak in
the fork of Georges Meadow, thence --- to the County line ---
to the main water course of Hutchen's Sw. ---,
16 Dec. 1714. The land was for the trans of:

John Nicholls	Tuch: Moore	Thomas Gvent
Hamaway (?) Hunt	ffrancis Cane	

  p. 198. Thomas Burge, 196 Acs., on both sides of Jones
Hole Sw. in Pr. Geo. Co., bounded: on the N. side of Jones
Hole Sw., thence --- 16 Dec. 1714 (The sd. land was for the)
Consideration of 20 s.

  p. 199. Mrs. Frances Wynne, Inq., Pr. Geo. Co., 150 Acs.,
(the index says 142 Acs., and so does the margin) escheated

from John ffarnham (?) dec'd., granted now to Mrs. ffrances Wynne, --- 142 Acs. in Pr. Geo. Co., on the S. side of Bayley's Cr., bounded: at the mouth of simson's gut --- to Wm. Roger's line, 16 Dec. 1714.

p. 221. John Evans, 1001 Acs., on the Stony Cr., Pr. Geo. Co., bounded: on the bank of the S. side of the sd. Cr. --- to a gum in a Br., thence down the same, 23 Dec. 1714. (There is no ref. to trans. and no list of names.)

John Eaton, p. 222, of York Co., 429 Acs. in Pr. Geo. Co., bounded: at a white oak on Southern Run in his line, (that(of?) George Blayton, dec'd.) thence along the sd. Blayton's Line --- being the course of Ralph Hill, thence --- 23 Dec. 1714. (The sd. land was for) trans. of: Matthihall(?) Markes
Mary Markes   Edw. Markes   John Markes
Harrett Markes   Sarah Markes   Wm. Tromsin(?)

p. 234. Nicholas Overby, 964 Acs., in Pr. Geo. Co., bounded: at a Butterwood on the watercourse of Leadbeter's Cr., thence --- to a small slash between 2 hickorys ---, 23 Dec. 1714. (The sd. land was for) trans. of:
Stephen Hix   Robt. Marlow   Mary Lar
Philip Burlett   Issac Garrett   Weary Middleton
Sarah Sihes   ffrancis Andrews   Edw. Stephens
Wm. Gaines   Leonard W(illia)mson   Thomas Harris
Ephraim Crafield(?)   Thomas Wilson   Lewis Loyd
Thomas Robins   Wm. Kefhill   John Lovet
                                             Barbara Warner

p. 241. Benjamine Evins, 81 Acs., in Pr. Geo. Co., bounded: at a corner hickory of Capt. Geo. Blayton dec'd., on his W. side -s (of?) Ponds Run, thence along the sd. Blaytons Lines ---, 16 Aug. 1715 & in consideration of 10 s.

p. 299. John Leadbiter, 100 Acs. on the S. side of Warwick Sw., in Pr. Geo. Co., adj. his old line, bounded: at a red oak, where William Temple lives, adj. sd. Leadbiter's ---, 1 Oct. 1716 & for consideration of 10 s.

p. 304. Joshua Prichard, 147 Acs., being on the S. side of Butterwood's Sw., in Pr. Geo. Co., bounded: on the sd. Sw. in Cedper (?) Run ---, 1 Oct. 1716, & in consideration of 15 s.

p. 304. William Gibbs, 82 Acs., on the N. side of Joseph Sw. adj. Epes' lines in the Co. of Pr. Geo., bounded: on the water course of the sd. Sw. --- to the Great Br. above the bridge in Puiaia(?) Road to Nottoway Riv., thence down the sd. Br. ---, 1 Oct. 1716 & in consideration of 10 s.

p. 309. Thomas Simmons, 299 Acs., on the N. side of Severed's(?) Sw., in Pr. Geo. Co., bounded: at his own line in the horse br, --- t0 a corner black oake of James Grentian, thence ---, 1 Oct. 1716 & in consideration of 30 s.

p. 309. Peter Wynne, 355 Acs., on the S. side of Butterwood Sw. in Pr. Geo. Co., bounded: at an elm at the intercourse thereof, below the Onominche Path ---, 31 Oct. 1716 & in consideration of 35 s.

p. 309. Nathaniel Tatum, 321 Acs., in Pr. Geo. Co. & bounded: at a corner hickory of Nath. Tatum Jr. on the S. side of Joseph's Sw., thence ---, 31 Oct. 1716 & in consideration of 35 s.

p. 309. Danashe Matone (the Index gives the first name as Daniel), 99 Acs., on both sides of Jones Hole Sw., Pr. Geo. Co., bounded: in the lwo ground on the N. side of the sd. Sw. ---, 31 Oct. 1716 & in consideration of 10 s.

p. 315. John Freeman, 431 Acs., in Pr. Geo. Co., bounded: on the N. side of Nottoway Riv. --- to the head of the reedy Br., thence down the same --- to Nottoway Riv., thence down Nottoway Riv. ---, 1 April 1717. The sum of 21 li. was the consideration.

p. 316. Abraham Heath, 151 Acs., on the S. side of Warwick Meadow, in Pr. Geo. Co., adj. the Co. line & bounded: in Samuel Tatum Sen'r's. line, which is crossed by the Co. line secure along the sd. Co. lines W. --- to Walker's line thence along the same ---, 1 April 1717 & in consideration of 15 s.

p. 319. Peter Lee, 112 Acs., on both sides of Warwick Sw., in Pr. Geo. Co., bounded: on the N. side of the sd. Sw. ---, 1 April 1717 & in consideration of 15 s.

p. 320. Edward Woodlief, 80 Acs., on the S. side of Warwick Sw., in Pr. Geo. Co., & bounded: on the S. side of the sd. Sw. --- to the water courses of the Warwick Sw., thence --- to the beginning, 1 April 1717 & in consideration of 10 s.

p. 320. Samuel Lee, 172 Acs., on the N. side of Warwick Sw., on the E. side of the Great Br. thereof, in Pr. Geo. Co. & bounded: on John Leadbiter's corner red oake --- to a corner of the side of a Br., thence N. --- to a Br. --- thence N. --- to John Leadbeater's line, thence along the same ---, 1 April 1717 & in consideration of 20 s.

p. 322. Nathaniel Tatum, 321 Acs., in Pr. Geo. Co. & bounded: on the S. side of Joseph's Sw., thence along his line S. --- to a chesnut oak in Joseph's Sw. about 4 po. below Dobys bridge, thence down the same --- to the beginning, 15 July 1717 & in consideration of 35 s.

p. 335. Richard Dearden, 100 Acs., on Lows Br., in Pr. Geo. Co., & bounded: on the E. side of the sd. Br., thence N. --- to the beginning, 15 July 1717 & in consideration of 10 s.

p. 335. John Strond, 46 Acs., on the S. side (of) Monofinech Cr., in Pr. Geo. Co. & bounded: in his line at a Br. on the E. side of his house, thence N. by W. --- to the beginning, 15 July 1717 & in consideration of 5 s.

p. 335. Maj. Robert Abernathy, 100 Acs., on the S. side of Lappons Cr., adj. to Maj. Robt. Mumford's Lands, in Pr. Geo. Co. & bounded: at a red oake in the sd. Mumford's line, thence W. --- along the sd. Mumford's Line, 15 July 1717 & in consideration of 10 s.

p. 335. Richard Smith Sr., 370 Acs., in Pr. Geo. Co., on the S. side of Lappons Cr. & bounded: on the lower side of the Br. (as the Ms.), thence S. --- to the beginning, 15 July 1717 & for trans. of:
Joseph Borne   Thomas Evans   John Penis
Benja: Brandriffe   John Hales   (all.)

p. 336. William Davis, 100 Acs on the S. side of Lappony Cr. on his own E. side of Horse pen Br., in Pr. Geo. Co. & bounded: at David Williams corner, thence binding upon the sd. William West --- to the beginning, 15 July 1717 & in consideration of 10 s.

p. 336. David Williams, 100 Acs. on the S. side of Lappony Cr., in Pr. Geo. Co., on the E. or lower side of horse pen Br. & bounded: above the Indian fiel(d)s, thence N. --- to the beginning, 15 July 1717 & in consideration of 10 s.

p. 336. Thomas Whood, 199 Acs. on both sides of a Br. of Nannisonds Cr., known by the name of Indian Br., below the River Path, in the Co. of Pr. Geo & bounded: on the W. side of the sd. Br., thence N. --- to a corner, thence E. to the beginning, 15 July 1717 & for trans. of 4 persons: John Moore   John Oughts   Richard Holland   Daniel Marshall

p. 336. Henry Michell Jr., 327 Acs., in Pr. Geo. Co. & bounded: on the watercourse of Jones Hole, thence W. --- on his Br., thence up the same --- to a corner --- on the water course of Jones Hole Sw., thence down the same --- to the beginning, 15 July 1717 & for trans of 7 persons:
Henry Mitchell   Thomas Apers   William Lewison
Joseph Hill   James Dinchoe   Mary Peades
                                          John Dixson

p. 337. Thomas Hobby, 198 Acs. on both sides of a Br. of Nannisonds Cr., known by the name of Indian Br., in Pr. Geo. Co. & bounded: below Nannisonds path on the W. side of the sd. Br., thence S. --- to a corner --- to the beginning, 15 July 1717 & in consideration of 20 s.

p. 337. Thompson Shapley, 200 Acs. on the N. side of Bear Sw., in Pr. Geo. no. & bounded: at a corner poplar in the sd. Sw. on the upper side of the upper great Br. above Onominche(?) path, thence S. --- to a Br., thence N. --- to the beginning, 15 July 1717 & in consideration of 20 s.

p. 337. Thomas Parrum, 54 Acs. on the S. side of Moccosoneck Cr., in Pr. Geo. Co. & bounded: in his own line where the same crosses Glany Quarter Br., thence along the same N. --- to the inter course of Glany Quarter Br., thence down the same --- to the beginning, 15 July 1717 & in consideration of 5 s.

p. 337. Richard Tally, 181 Acs. on the S. side of Appamattox Riv., in Pr. Geo. Co. & bounded: on the Br. of Appamattox Riv. below Wombapock fford, thence S. --- to a gum on Appamattox Riv., thence up the same --- to the beginning, 15 July 1717 & in consideration of 20 s.

p. 337. Thomas Clay, 100 Acs. on the W. side of Namasond Cr. & on the W. side of the great Br. there parallel to the River Path, in Pr. Geo. Co. & bounded: at a corner hickory between his sd. path & a meadow, thence E. ---, 15 July 1717 & in consideration of 10 s.

p. 338. Charles Williams Jr., 197 Acs. on the S. side of the Second Sw., in Pr. Geo. Co. & bounded: on the S. side of the Ashen Br., thence W. --- 15 July 1717 & in consideration of 20 s.

p. 338. John Tucher, 200 Acs. on the E. side of Namusend Cr., in Pr. Geo. Co. & bounded: on the E. side of Ellingtons Br., thence N. ---, 15 July 1717 & in consideration of 20 s. (For Tucher, compare Tucker, Bk. 10, p. 339.)

p. 338. Thomas Jones, son of Richard Jones, 247 Acs. at the head of Great Cr. of Nottoway Riv. on the N. side of it, in Pr. Geo. Co. & bounded: at a corner red oak in the fork of the sd. Cr., thence E. ---, 15 July 1717 & in consideration of 25 s.

p. 338. William Pettypoole, 65 Acs. on the S. side of Moccosoneck Cr., in Pr. Geo. Co. & bounded: at a red oak in his own line, thence S. ---, 15 July 1717 & in consideration of 10 s.

p. 338-9. Francis Coleman Sr., 333 Acs. on the S. side of Butterwood Sw. or Cr., in Pr. Geo. Co.

& bounded: near the mouth of a small Br., thence S. --- an oak by the side of a small Br., thence E. --- to a butterwood on the main water course of butterwood Sw. or Cr., thence up the same, ---, 15 July 1717 & in consideration of 35 s.

p. 339. John Ellington, 200 Acs. on both sides of Ellingtons Br. of Namusonds Cr., in Pr. Geo. Co. & bounded: on the W. side of the sd. Br., thence S. ---, 15 July 1717 & in consdieration of 20 s.

p. 339. William Coleman Sr., 100 Acs. on the W. side of Namusonds Cr. on the W. side of a Great Br. which runs parrallell to the River Path, in Pr. Geo. Co. & bounded: in Joseph Tuchers line, thence E. ---, 15 July 1717 & in consideration of 10 s.

p. 339. Francis Tucker Sr., 289 Acs. on both sides of Mawhipponock Cr., in Pr. Geo. Co. & bounded: on the watercourse of the Great Br. of the sd. Cr. on the E. side thereof, thence N. --- on the W. side of the sd. Cr., thence along the same & S. after the course of E. --- to Herbert's line, 15 July 1717 & in consideration of 30 s.

p. 339. Richard Smith Sr., 83 Acs. on the S. side of Moccosoneck Cr., adj. his own Land, in Pr. Geo. Co. & bounded: in his own line --- to Parrums line, thence N. --- to a corner dividing the sd. Parram & Smith, thence along Smiths line W. ---,

15 July 1717 & in consideration of 10 s.

p. 340. Robert Tucker, 141 Acs. on the W. side of Namusond Cr. & on the W. side of the Great Br., thereof, In Pr. Geo. Co. & bounded: on the S. side of a Br. of the sd. Great Br., thence E. ---, 15 July 1717 & in consideration of 15 s.

p. 340. William Rives, 206 Acs. on the S. side of Nottoway Riv., in Pr. Geo. Co. & bounded: on the bank of the sd. Riv. & upon the bank of the sd. Riv., thence down the Riv. ---, 15 July 1717 & for trans of:
Anne Rockwell   Arthur Stamp   Isabell Burrough
                   Ruth Ivie   John Howard

p. 340. John Tally, 300 Acs. on the S. side of Appomattox Riv., above the mouth of Namusond Cr., in Pr. Geo. Co. & bounded: on the bank of the sd. Riv., thence down to same ---, 15 July 1717 & in consideration of 30 s.

p. 341. John Fountain & Robert Wynn, 175 Acs. on the S. side of Joseph Sw., in Pr. Geo. Co. & bounded: on the watercourse of the sd. Sw. --- in the line of Nathaniel Tatum Jr., thence along his line --- on the watercourse of Joseph Sw., thence down the same ---, 15 July 1717 & for trans of 4 persons:
Thomas Blichendint   John Bunchley
Rich. With__(two letters unreadable)nke   John Jones

p. 341. Nathaniel Tatum Jr., 221 Acs. in Pr. Geo. Co. & bounded: at a corner hickory of the sd. Tatum, thence, along his own line N. --- to a black oak of Samll. Tatum Jr., thence along his line E. ---, 15 July 1717 & in consideration of 25 s.

p. 342. William Caleb, 119 Acs. on the S. side of Blackwater Sw. in Pr. Geo. Co. & bounded: at a corner white oak of Mr. John Nichols in the fork of Georges Meadow, thence S. --- to the County line, thence along the same W. --- to Benja: Fosters line in the fork of a Br. of Georges Meadow, thence down the sd. Br. ---, 15 July 1717 & for trans. of 3 persons:
Martha stwarter(?)   Eliza. Peebles   Philip Burrough

p. 348. in consideration of 25 s., to Shanes Haynes, 230 Acs. on the N. side of Jones Hole Sw., in Pr. Geo. Co. & bounded: at Thomas Raynes corner above his house, thence E. --- on the watercourse of Jones Hole Sw., thence down the same --- to Bobbetts line --- to Rayner's alias Paces line, thence along the same N. --- 22 Jan. 1717 (probably 1717/18.)

p. 349. William Raines, of Pr. Geo. Co., 400 Acs. on both sides of Little Cr., in Surry Co. & bounded: by the Cr. side, thence N. --- to a white oak by the side of Little Cr. aforesd., just above the mouth of a small Br., thence up it ---, 22 Jan. 1717(1717/1718 probably) & in consideration of 40 s.

p. 363. James Baugh Jr. & Henry Mayes, 283 Acs. on the N. side of the Second Sw., in Pr. Geo. Co. & bounded: at a corner red oak of Danll Nindivant & James Hall, thence W. ---, 24 Jan. 1717(-18 probably) & for trans. of 6 persons:
Peter Hall   Elizabeth Downing Jr.   Eliza. Agar
Christopher Nedrent   John McCray   Thomas Massey

p. 365. George Passmore & John Peterson, 225 Acs., on the S. side of Nottoway Riv., in Pr. Geo. Co. & bounded: on the Riv., thence S. --- to a Sassafras on the Br. of Nottoway Riv., thence down the same ---, 18 March 1717(-18 probably) & in consideration of 20 s. & for trans of 1 person, Alexander Notos

p. 367. John Evans, 175 Acs on the S. side of Stony Cr., in Pr. Geo. Co. & bounded: on the water course of the sd. Cr., thence W. to Stony Cr., thence up the same ---, 18 March 1717 (-18 probably) & in consideration of 20 s.

p. 400. Christopher Roberson, 115 Acs. on the N. side of the white Oak Sw., in Pr. Geo. Co. & bounded: on the water course of the sd. Sw., thence N. --- to the intercourse of the sd. White Oak Sw., thence down the same, ---, 15 July 1718 & in consideration of 15 s.

p. 401, Abraham Jones. of Pr. Geo. Co., 141 Acs. on the N. side of Nottoway River in the sd. Pr. Geo. Co. & bounded: on Peter Jones Jr.'s line thence N. --- to the sd. Riv., thence up the same ---, 14 July 1718 & in consideration of 15 s.

p. 401. John Davis, 400 Acs., in Pr. Geo. Co. on the W. side of Wallis's Cr. & bounded: on the W. side of Wallis's Cr. at a hickory marked 4 ways in the line of Nicholas Overby, thence S. ---, 14 July 1718 & in consideration of 40 s.

p. 401. William Anderson, 299 Acs. on both sides of Mawhippanock Cr., in Pr. Geo. Co. & bounded: at Matthew Mayes Upper corner on the W. side of the sd. Cr., thence W. --- to a corner near the upper Namusond Pathe, thence N. ---, 14 July 1718 & in consideration of 30 s.

p. 402. William Westbrooke, 100 acs., on the S. side of the White Oak Sw., in Pr. Geo. Co. & below the Occomoneck Path & bounded: on the S. side of the sd. Sw., thence S. ---, 14 July 1718 & in consideration of 10 s.

p. 402. Matthew Mayes, 398 ½ Acs. on both sides of Mawhippanock Cr., in Pr. Geo. Co. & bounded: at a corner red oak in the fork of Squabling Br., being the Br. of the sd. Cr. between the plantations of the sd. May:s and William Anderson, thence N. ---, 14 July 1718 & for trans. of 8 per sons:
Edward Baker   Wm. Wilson   Robt. Owen   Jno. Johnson
Henry Hill   John Jugles   Eliza: Parker   Eliza: Kendall

p. 402. Henry Mayes, 200 Acs on both sides of Mawhippaneck Cr., in Pr. Geo. Co. & bounded: in the line of ffrancis Tucker, thence W. --- in ffrancis Tucker's line, thence along the same S. ---, 14 July 1718 & for trans of 4 persons:
Edw. Crowder   Eliza: Taylor   Dan. Hurly   Benja: Black

p. 402. Joseph Tucker, 403 Acs. on both sides of Stony Cr., in Pr. Geo. Co. & bounded: on the S. side of the sd. Cr. at an oak on the S. side of the sd. Cr. at an oak standing on the bank thereof, thence W. --- to the mouth of a gutt on the N. of the sd. Cr., thence up the sd. gutt or Br. --- to a corner gum of

Capt. Jno. Evans, thence along the sd. Evans line E. --- to Wm. Tuckers line, thence along the same W. --- on the bank of Stony Br., thence down the same ---, 14 July 1718 & in considerationof 40 s.

p. 403, John Lewis, 251 Acs. on the N. side of Nottoway Riv. on the upper side of Buckskin Cr., in Pr. Geo. Co. & bounded: at the mouth of the sd. Cr., thence up the same --- to the corner gum at the mouth of a dry gully, thence E. --- to a small holly tree on the sd. Riv. bank at the mouth of a small dry gully, thence down the sd. Riv. ---, 14 July 1718 & in consideration of 25 s.

p. 403. Robert Mumford, of Pr. Geo. Co., 592 Acs. on the S. side of Moccosoneck Cr., in the sd. Pr. Geo. Co. & bounded: beg. in the Co. line on the S. side of the Sd. Cr., thence W. --- to an ash in the Reedy Br., thence down the sd. Br. --- to Moccosoneck Cr., thence down the same ---, 14 July 1718 & in consideration of 3 li.

p. 403. Peter Michell Jr., ofPr. Geo. Co., 142 Acs. on the N. side of Nottoway Riv., in Pr. Geo. Co. & bounded: at an oak on the Riv. above the Piny Pond, thence E. --- to Nottoway Riv., thence down the same ---, 14 July 1718 & in considerationof 15 s.

p. 446. Robert Mumford, 390 Acs. on the W. side of horse pen Br. & on the S. side of Lappone Cr., in Pr. Geo. Co. & bounded: at a corner hickory, thence N. ---, 11 July 1719 & in considerationof 40 s.

p. 446. William Tucker of Pr. Geo. Co., 143 Acs. on the N. side of Stony Cr., in the sd. Pr. Geo. Co. & bounded: at a holly on the bank of the sd. Cr. in the Co. line, thence E. --- to Stony Cr., thence down the same ---, 11 July 1719 & for trans. of 2 persons & for s s.:
John Voyer & Jane his wife

End of the Pr. Geo. Co. Land Patents in Book 10

Index to Names in the Land Patents, Books 6-10 inclusively for the
Counties of Charles City (S. side only) and to
those of Prince George County.

Note: The pages given are to those of the text.

Abernathy, Robert 7;338; 10:335
Abett, John 9:395
Able, Anne 10:198
Ablesone, Isa 7:332
Adams, Addams, Geo. 7:331;
  Jno. 6:488, 510
Addison, Xopher 7:124
Adeer, Xpher 7:633
Adoar, Xopher 8:244
Adington, Edward 7:150
Agar, Eliz. 10:363
Aker, Corn. 9:395
Aldus, Fra. 9:711
  Wm. 9:711
Alee, John 8:111, 9:394
Alford, Tho. 6:529
  Alice 9:2
Allaman, Hen. 6:510
Allen, Allin, Arthur 8:127;
  174, 175, 325-519
  Ja. 8:78; 9:325-519
  Jno. 6:510
  Robt. 8:57
Allett, John 7:124
Alley, Henry 7:654
Allester, Edward 6:85
Alson, Tho. 6:510
Anderson, _ 6:480
  David 6:480
  Inghambed 6:529
  John 9:715
  Reginald 7:192
  Reynard 7:709
  Sam. 8:173
  Tho. 6:182; 488; 7:303;
    10:144
  Wm. 8:368; 10:401
Andrews, David 8:75
  Francis 10:234
  Lydia (;461
  Wm. 10:402
Angell, Wm. 9:391
Annimer, Patrick 9:742
Annitt, Edd. 6:553
Apers, Tho. 10:336
Appleby, Jas. 8:75
Arch, Tho. 6:613
Archer, Capt. 7:332, 488;
  Geo. 7:331
Armefield, Lyida 10:40
Armstrong, Armestrong, Geo.
  6:39
  Henry &;164; 512
  John 6:327
  Wm. 9:391
Armstead, Anne 9:714
Arnold, Eliz. 6:480
  Niche 9:714
  Wm. 7:335
Arrengo__, Wm. 8:123
Arthur, Gabriel 8:111
Ashday, Kiddy 6:488
Ashley, Aylse 6:488
  Robt. 9:407
  Tho 9:525
Ashton, James 8:76
  Robt. 8:111
Atkins, Chester 7:331
  James 6:480
  Jonathon 9:382
Atkinson, Rich. 164
Auborne, Jon 7:335
Avery, Judith 6:227
  Mark 6:326

Babcock, James 7:328
Badd, John 9:525
Bagwell, Tho. 7:339
Baker, Edw. 10:402
  John 6:203
  Job 6;330
  Millicent 8:75
Ball, Jno. 6:227
  Law. 9:706
  Mary 9:714
  Wm. 9:388
Ballingster, Margt. 8:71
Baltamore, Henry 9:2
Bannister, Banister, _, wife
  of John 8:80
  John 8:80, 111; 10:125, 198
Bankse, Bankes, Geo. 6:446
  Mary 7:138
Barcley, Fra. 7:332
Bardoe, Jno. 6:227
Barker, Hannah 9:715
  Joane 8:71
  Wm. 6:480; 8:71
Barlor, Barlow & see Barlow,
  John 8:244
Barlow & see Barlor, Jno.
  6:480; 9:394
  Han. 6:480
  Robt. 9:480
Barnes, John 9:494
  Robt. 7:246
Barrel, Tho. 303
Barrey, Jno. 9:391
Barrow, Hugh 6:227
  Tho. 7:303
Bartholemew, Chas 9:572
Bartlett, Cha. 6:510
Bas(e), Geo. 7:663; 8:244
  Rich. 8:244
Bateman, Athony 9:706
Bates, Mr. 9:656
  Henry 7:150
  Rich 8:369
Battice, John 9:711
Batt(s), Capt. 6:203
  Mr. 7:583
  Henry 6:446, 480, 484, 486;
    7:335, 469, 708; 8:57,
    174, 368, 411; 9:711;
  Tho. 6:484; 7:45
  Wm. 6:285; 8:173
Battow, Wm. 7:30
Baugh, James 10:363 (Jr.)
Baxter, Jno. 8:16_(?)
Bayford, Jacob 9:451
Bayley, Edw. 9:523
  Jacob 7:305
Beale, Andrew 8:75
Beazley, Robt. 7:199; 9:2
Beddwick, James 9:494
Bell, Geo. 7:335
  Roger 7:244
Bellamy, Ja. 8:77
Belnett, Wm. 6:134
Benford, Geo. 9:714
  Tho. 9:714
Beningon, Tho. 7:45
Benn, Ed. 9:714
Bennett, Mary 6:182; 8:71
  Robt. 6:62
  Tho. 10:77
Bently, Wm. 8:174
Berry, Anne 8:111
  Connie 9:394
  Gowen 8:111
  Robt. 7:274

Berry, Cont.
  Sarzel 6:134
Bernard, Wm. 6:510
Besse, John 7:654
Bevins, Jno. 7:45
Bibiell, Joyce 9:572
Bines, Hep. 9:395
Binforte, Binford, Jas.
  7:338; 10:125
Binly, Jno. 8:369
Birchett, Bircherd, Edw.
  6:446, 486; 7:29,
  535, 708
Bird, Byrd, Mr. 6:142; 406;
  9:189
  Edw. 7:285
  Frank 6:529
  James 6:85
  John 6:134
  Wm. 9:291, 393, 396, 397,
    406, 420, 439, 493, 494,
    519, 571, 572, 582, 656,
    742
  see Mr. Auditor
Bishop, Bushop, John 7:305,
  306
Bisse, James 7:564
Bittern, Robt. 7:192
Black, Ben. 10:402
Blacksho, Jno. 7:45
Blag, John 9:157
Blake, Renne 7:45
Blamore, James 7:124
Bland, Rich 9:711; 9:718
  (2 Patents.)
Blayton, Geo. 10:222; 241
Blichendint, Tho. 10:341
Blight 9:656
Blighton, Mr. 8:77;
  Geo. 9:225
Blunt, Tho. 8:371; 9:325-519;
  10:178
Boakley, Robt 8:71
Bobbett, _ 10:348
Bolling, Bo(w)l(1)in(g),
  Robt. 7:199, 535; 8:77,
  104, 106; 9:85, 298,
  398, 493, 571, 714
Bollitt, Rebecka 9:2
Bond, Hen. 7:330
Bonner, Mary 6:447
Bonogline, Florence 9:391
Bonus, Timo. 9:716
Booth, Jean 7:124;
  Rich. 9:706
Borar, Borer, Jane 7:199;
  9:2
Boreman 9:397
Borne, Joseph 10:335
Borrow, Jno. 8:244
Bottomly, Ellinur 6:446
Bourgh, Margt. 9:461
Bourne, Robt. 7:237
  Wm. 7:510
Bow, Anth. 7:331
Bowley, Phill. 6:480
Bowman, Edw. 9:711
Boydson, Isaac 7:305
Boyle 9:742
Bradley, Dor. 7:338
  Fra. 7:330
Bradshaw, Adam 6:510
  Arnold 9:461
  Ja. 6:480
Branch, Rebecca 8:106
  Xpler 7:339

Brandriffe, Benja. 10:335
Brannard, Wm. 6:480
Branstone, Tho. 7:338
Bray, John 9:391
Brechinhead, Rase. 6:480
Brett, Wm. 6:480
Brichett, Edw. 7:45
Bridger, Joseph 9:325-519
Bride(s), Chas. 9:325-519
  Anne 9:525
  Law., 9:451
  Susanna 7:124
Brimble, Henry 10:40
Brise, Rich 6:480
Britton, Lyon 7:199
  Mary 9:380
Brocke(s), John 10:51
  Tho. 9:388
Bromeley, Rich. 7:122
Brooke(s), Jer. 8:71
  Margt. 9:715
  Nich. 7:45
  Sisley 7:285
  Walter 6:203; 327; 9:85
Brothers 9:395
Browne, Anne 6:529
  Chris. 6:289
  Eliz. 7:335; 9:391
  James 7:306; 8:71
  John 6:510
  Mary 6:510; 7:244; 9:461
  Moll. 6:480
  Oreginall 9:157
  Rich 7:199
  Susanna 9:461
  Tho. 6:529; 9:391, 714
  Wm. 6:480, 529; 7:124; 8:111
    9:325-519
  John 10:51
Bruce, Rich. 7:336
  Sanders 8:111
Brumfeild, John 9:388
  Eliz. 9:572
Brus, Sanders 7:45
Brush, Wm. 6:62
Bryan, Derby 9:391
  Margt. 9:706
Bucher, Tho. 8:173
Buck, Steph. 7:328
Buckley, John 9:157
Bull, John 8:149
Bulmer, Ben. 7:339
Bunchley, John 10:341
Bupton, Sam. 8:111
Burcher, _ 9:676
Burdges, Robt. 8:218
Burefoy, Sam 9:705
Burer, Geo. 7:124
Burge, Tho. 10:198
Burgesse, Burges, _ 7:30
  Jno. 6:510
  Robt. 6:39, 509; 7:30
Burgaine, John 6:480
Burke, Tho. 9:742
Burlett 10:234
Burrage, John 6:480
Burrough, Isabell 10:340
  Phil 10: 342
Burton, John 9:407
  Tho. 9:714
  Wm. 9:391
Busby, Capt. 7:122
  Mary 7:657
  Robt. 6:273
  Tho. 6:273; 7:407, 657
    9:380, 388, 399
Bush, Adam 8:123
  Sarah 8:123
Bushell, Anne 8:173
  Mary 8:173
  Robt. 8:411
  Tho. 8:173
Butler, Ed. 7:332; 9:742

Butler, Cont.
  John 6:488; 8:71; 9:388,
    407, 714; 10:51
  Mary 9:388
  Mutus 9:714
  Rich. 9:391
  Wm. 6:510

Cabbock, Ja. 6:227
Caddy, Rich. 9:391
Cailer, Dennis 9:380
Cairlike, Rich. 7:272
Cake, Rich. 6:553
Calcutt, Mary 9:388
Calloway, Tho. 6:246
Cane, Francis 10:198
Cann, James 7:164
Canter, Wm. 7:543; 8:267
For Cappell, see Chappell
Cappoke, Ja. 6:480
Carder, Step. 9:391
Cardy, Hugh 7:246
Care, Dan 6:480
Carlisle, Rich 8:370; 9:493
Carman, Ellinor 9:742
Carrill, Carroll, Jno. 9:391
  Rich. 7:285
Carter, Math. 8:75
Carty, Sarah 9:742
Oarver, Jno. 8:75
Cary, Edward 8:75
Case, Robt. 8:71
Catthill, James 8:244
Chamberlin, Maj. 8:76
  Tho. 8:38
Chandler, Francis 6:85
Chanus, Hen. 7:30
Chapfeild, Jane 9:407
Chapell, Capell, Tho. 7:332,
  339, 488; 8:77, 371;
  9:460, 493; 10:178;
  9:189
Chaphan, Mary 8:71
Chapman, Tho. 9:388
Chaplin, _ 7:531
Charles, Tho. 7:543, 654
Cheeseman, Hen. 7:244
Chena, Prisila 6:488 & see
  below
Chenye, Priscilla 7:124 &
  see above
Child, Fra. 7:45
Childers, Philemon 6:481
Chiles, Walter 6:189; 7:339
Chilton, Edw. 8:75
Chiswell, Edw. 7:271
City, Fra. 8:369
Clark, Cath. 8:368
  Eliz. 8:218, 369
  Hen. 7:575
  Rich 7:512
  Tho. 6:510
Clause, Benetha 9:2
Clay, Jas. 9:395
  John 8:368
Clayton, Geo. 8:369
  Mary 8:75
Cleavley, Fra. 9:2
Clenck, Hen. 8:71
Clerke, Robt. 9:395
  Sarah 9:714
Cob, Andrew 7:657
Cobutt, Wm. 7:24
Coby, Jane 9:451
Cocke, James 8:60, 71, 369;
  9:420
  Step. 9:224
Cocken, Wm. 8:71
Cocklin, Alice 8:71
Cocobill, Geo. 9:2
Coebb, Mary 10:51
Cole, Jon 7:335

Cole, Cont.
  Sarah 7:339
  Tho. 6:247
Coleman, _, 6:62; 8:218
  Francis 10:338-9
  Robt. 6:39, 134, 189, 447;
    7:30, 46; 6:286
  Wm. 10:339
Colery, Eliz. 6:39
Collagham, Cornel. 9:391
Collyer, Isabell 9:714
Colliford, Charles 9:525
Collin(g)s, Anne 654
  Avis 7:654
  John 6:484
Colson, _, 7:30
Combe, Rich. 488
Competon, Tho. 9:2
Cond, Jeffry 7:657
Conniers, Dennis 7:328
  Math. 9:391
Connell, John 9:706
  Tim. 9:391
Conner, John 9:391
Con(a)way, Fra. 7:45
  Jon 7:335
Cooke, Edw. 7:253
  Fra. 9:711
  Giles 7:328
  Ja. 8:35
  Robt. 6:182
  Wm. 9:711
Cooper, Ann 7:272
  Ed. 7:306
  Eliz. 6:510
  Jon 7:335
  Mary 7:275
  Sarah 9:714
  Tho. 6:529
  Wm. 7:535
Cooslime, Edm. 9:391
Corbin, Eliza 9:494
Corder, Natha. 7:332
Corne, Tho. 9:742
Cosby, Andrew 8:75
Cotterell, Rose 9:391
Couneley, Patrick 9:572
Courser, Sam 9:2
Covey, Robt. 9:2
Cowherd, James 10:198
Cox, Jno. 6:510
Crafford, David 8:75
Crafield(?), Ephraim 10:234
Cranage, Ed. 7:332
Crawshaw, Rich. 6:62
Crayford, Randall 8:75
Creede, Robt. 8:76
Creneds, Ja. 6:480
Crew, And. 6:510
  Jno. 6:510
Cribis, Tho. 6:488
Crickett, Ren. 7:275
Crinly, Robt. 7:274
Crockson, _, 9:676
Crod, Robt. 8:57
Crompton, Tho. 6:481
Cromwell, Jno. 6:227
Crondon, Henry 7:654
Crooke, Solomon 8:60, 218
Cropey, Tho. 7:330
Crosland, Geo. 7:335
Cross(e), Cath. 6:446
  Rich. 10:40
Crowder, Barth. 9:291
  Edw. 10:402
  Wm. 6:480
Crowther, Robt. 9:711
Crump, Jno. 8:244
Cumber, John 6:484
Cunitton, Tho. 192
Curtis, John 9:494
Cuteley, Francis 6:85
Cutson, Rich. 6:480

Daglas, John 8:244
Danby, Ann 6:227
Dance, Geo. 9:380
Daniell, Jno. 8:123
　Sarah 9:461
Dare, Edw. 9:394
Dart, Geo. 9:391
Davenport, Oliver 6:488
David, a Scotchman 6:227
Davies, Hugh 9:2
　Wm. 8:111
Davis, Duke 9:525
　Geo. 6:286
　Issabella 9:706
　Johan 6:480
　John 6:488; 8:111; 10:401
　Margt. 9:395
　Mary 6:446; 9:525
　Tho. 6:85
　Wm. 9:391, 461; 10:336
Davison, Alexander 8:370; 7:285
Dawes, Ann 7:271, 275
Deane, Matt. 9:714
Deardon, Rich 10:335
Dearelove, Rich. 6:480
Decus, John 9:715
Deering, Jno. 8:74
Deucely, Anth. 9:706
Dennis, Rich. 6:510
Denson, Wm. 7:332
Dent, James 6:289, 317
Deon, John 9:711
Dickson, Dickeson, Dixon,
　Dickenson, Anne 9:461
　Joan 7:328
　John 10:336
　Tho. 8:76
Dinchoe, James 10:336
Dison, Nath. 8:111
Ditty, Wm. 6:285; 8:173, 411;
　9:438
Doby, John 9:125; see Doby
　Bridge
Dodd, Rich. 10:66
Don_kin, 4__, 9:391
Donavaine, Dan. 9:391
Donklin, Jno. 8:411
Donnell, Dommat 6:553
Donaghene, Kath. 9:391
Doran, Louge 9:391
Dorrell, John 6:488
Doughtye, Abrah. 8:77
　Mary 9:393
Douse, Tho. 9:711
Dowling, John 9:391
Downes, Hester 8:174
Downing, Eliz. 6:480;
　10:363
　Wm. 6:480
Dradge, Wm. 8:369
Dransell, Mary 6:529
Drayton, John, Jr. 7:285
Dreg, Roger 9:742
Drew, John 9:391
　Mary 8:111; 9:461
　Tho. 6:613
Drin, Mary 9:397
Duberly, Eliz 9:461
Duck, Eliz. 9:394
Duglis, Alice 9:395
Duncomb, Harbertt 9:157
Dunn, Rich. 9:711
　Tho. 9:391
Durell (or Duwell), Nich.
　8:55
Durrant, James 6:289, 317
Dyasmond, Robt. 6:327
Dyer, Eliz. 6:480

Earley, Adam 8:76
　Patrick, Earne 9:706
Easleton, Geo. 9:714
Eaton, Eliza. 10:51

Eaton, Cont.
　John 10:222
Edloo, Jno. 7:122
Edmonds, Edmunds, Wm. 7:124,
　150, 270, 331, 553; 9:656
Eennys 9:714, Matt. Eennys.
Egdole, Dorothy 7:46
Eggerton, Jno. 8:111
Elizer, Jona 7:331
Ellett, Jno. 8:411
Ellington, John 10:339
Elliett, Peter 8:75
Ellis, Elles, Edw. 6:227,
　Han(n)ah 7:543
　John 7:489; 8:75, 111;
　　9:224
　Lawr. 6:227
　Mary 7:122
　Robt. 8:75
　Sampson 7:335
Ellmer, Zach. 6:65
　Elmer, Abra. 8:74
Elsby, Susanna 8:74
Ely, Jane 10:51
Elson, Robt. 8:123
Emerson, Jane 8:77
Emons, Wm. 6:273
England, Wm. 9:714
English, John 9:388
Epes, Epps, Maj. 6:481;
　10:144, 304
　Francis 6:39, 62, 203;
　　9:380, 493
　John 6:39, 62
Evans, Abra. 9:325-519
　Ben. 9:663; 10:241
　Edwan 9:224
　Evan 9:224
　Griffeth 6:480
　John 7:216, 543; 8:71, 75,
　　369; 9:2; 10:221, 367,
　　402
　Robt. 7:150
　Tho. 10:335
Everett, Ruth 8:78
Ewens, John 7:30

Fairbrother, Susan 6:488
Fairclots, Ellen 6:488
Fan, John 9:380
Farlor, James 6:447
Farmon, Rich. 9:451
Farnham, (?), John 10:199
Farmouth, Jno. 7:55
Farrar, Mr. 7:24
　Margtt. 7:45
　Wm. 6:509
Farrell, Mary 9:391
Faulner, An. 6:447
Fells, Joseph 7:303
Feldome, Wm. 332
Fenly, Robt. 8:411
Fenns, Mary 8:411
Ferick, Hump. 6:62
Ferne, Law. 9:742
Festervill, Testervill, Lugy
　8:106
Fiffett, Robt. 7:331
Finch, Fra. 7:338
Fisher, Dan 9:395
Fitchett, Tho. 6:227
Flahaven, Rich 10:151
Flanagin, James 10:40
Flattman, Tho. 9:706
Fleming, Wm. 7:45
Fling, Kath. 9:706
Flood, Hercules 6:447, 510
　Jon 7:335, 338
　Mary 7:45
　Hercules 7:469; 8:55, 57;
　　9:571, 711
Florenor, Eliza 9:711
Florine, Tohnasin 6:510

Floyd, Jno. 6:510; 9:706
　Tho. 7:328
Ford, Eliner 8:71
Forest, Wm. 7:583
Fosler, Wm. 7:583
Fosler, Pat. 9:2
Foster, Ben. 7:273, 322;
　9:582; 10:51, 342
Fountain, John 10:341
Fowke, Ellener 6:227
Fox, John 9:714
Franklin, Judeth 8:211
Freame, John 6:246
Freeman, John 9:397; 10:315
　Mary 9:397
Freese, Edw. 9:494
Frith, Elm. 6:62
Frout, Peter 7:199
Fry, James 7:512
　Kath. 6:480
　Peregrin 9:298
Fucket, Gill 9:2
Fuller, John 9:461
　Furbush 8:367
Furbush, Jane 8:367
Furing, Anne 9:714
Fury, James 9:391

Gage, Wm. 7:338
Gainer, Good(man?) 10:51
Gaines, John 9:742
　Wm. 10:234
Galel, Wm. 7:237
Gant 7:332, Rich. Gant
Gardnere, Anth. 6:39
　Rich 7:332
Garrett, Isaac 10:234
Gatersone, Wm. 7:122
Gates, Jno. 9:2
Gauler, Ganter, Henry 7:543;
　8:106, 211
Gaville, John 7:46
Gaury, Wm. 7:583
Favsey, Chris 6:529
Gay, Walter 6:480
Gayer, Sampson 9:742
Gent, Tho. 7:339; 8:111
George, John 9:439
　Morice 6:480
　Rebecca 9:451
Gibbons, Mary 6:182
Gibbs, Martha 6:510
　Wm. 304
Gibson, Jon. 7:339
Gilbert, Wm. 9:461
Gilbert, Wm. 9:461
Giles, Job 9:378
　Tho. 9:325-519
Gill, Wm. 7:339
Gillereast 9:380
　Robt. Gillereast
Gillom, Hinsha 9:325-519
　Jno. 8:25
Gilson, Eliza 9:380
　Tho. 8:77
Glandon, Robt. 9:391
Gledger, Phil. 6:480
Goad, Francis 8:111
Godfrey, Ann 6:488
　Vincent 9:380
Gold, Jon 7:339
Golding, Jon 7:237
Goldin, Nath 8:71
Gollighty, John 7:663; 8:660
Good(s), Mr. 7:512
　David 6:510
　Adam 8:77
Goodale, David 6:510
Goodrich, Bisard (or Edward)
　10:66
　Chas. 7:553; 9:656
　Edward (or Bisard) 10:66
Gordon, Wm. 8:77

Gorman, Phil 6:488
Gotham, Tho. 7:633
Goton, Tho. 8:244
Gotterple, Vinc. 9:388
Gourd, Rich 9:339, 395
Gowen, _, 6:62
Gower, Edw. 7:199
  Tho. 7:199
Graine, Martin 6:553
Grant, Ann 7:45
  Mary 9:391
Grantham, Grantian, Jer. 9:742
  James 10:309
Gras, Roger 7:657
Graveley, Jone, 7:335
Graves (or Granes), John 6:529
Grea, Wm. 8:174
Greene, Edw. 7:512
  Eliz. 8:75
  Gerard 6:85
  Lewis 9:438, 705
Greeson, Jas. 9:718
  Wm. 10:197
Greenwood, Edward 6:404
Gretion, 9:380
Grice, Tho. 6:85
Griffin, Hugh 6:480
Griffith, Rich. 8:369; 9:395
Grimshaw, John 6:289
Grogerine, Tho. 6:510
Grymes, Derry 6:327
Guy, Sarah 7:274
Gyent 10:198

Haines, Robt. 8:75
Hales, Anth. 9:525
  John 10:335
Haley, Robt. 6:480
Hall, Anne 7:328
  Hannah 8:75
  Instance 9:87
  James 7:24; 8:411
  John 9:716
  Peter 10:363
  Steph. 7:328
  Susanna 8:75
Hambleton, Kath. 9:391
  Sarah 9:391
  Tho. 8:75
Hamer, Rich. 7:331
Hamlyn, Hamblin, John 8:370; 9:9:656
Hambrok, Henry 9:742
Hammond, Xopher 7:332
Hanakin, Edw. 6:480
Hand, Margt. 9:742
Hanks, Wm. 10:198
Hannon, Tho. 8:77
Hardiman, John 9:714, 718
Harley, Dan 9:716
Harmon, Henry 7:305
Harnison, Tho. (the first name is omitted from the text, so a correction) 9:460; see Harnson
Harnold, Joh. 7:199
Harnson, Mary 8:244
  Tho. 9:325-519
Harrington, Wm. 7:407
Harris, John 7:237, 246, 339; 8:57; 9:125
  Tho. 10:234
  Wm. 6:85; 9:525, 711
Harrison, Ben. 9:706, 740
  Eliz or Eliza 9:2
  Nath. 9:325-519
  Robt. 7:45; 9:706
  Wm. 6:86, 246; 7:330, 657, 8:78
  Harry 9:125
Harry 9:125
Harry, Geo. 9:391

Harry, Cont.
  Sampson 9:224
Harwood, Arthur 7:564
  Rich. 8:75
  Simon 6:480
Hartwell, Ed. 7:332
  Henry 7:130, 175
Harvey, Priscilla 10:51
Hasket, Anth. 8:111
Hatchman, Jane 9:711
Hatfield, John 10:198
Hatter, Geo. 7:150
Hatton, Geo. 8:244
Hawgood, Fra. 6:289, 317
Hawkes, Jeffery 9:388
Hawthorn, Robt. 9:394
Hay, Gilbert 7:124
Hayes, Eliz 335
Haynes, David 7:335
  Ralph 7:575
  Shanes 10:348
Hayward, Ellen 7:339
  Wm. 7:339
Heath, Abra 9:676; 10:316
  Adam 9:676
Helbert, Ellinor 9:742
Hellon, Jon 7:330
Hemsteed, Hannah 7:138
Henley, Sarah 7:335
Herbert, _, 10:339
  David 9:391
  Ed. 7:328
  John 8:75, 75; 9:2, 291, 451
Herd, Eliz. 6:488
  Susan 7:543
Hewgille, Wm. 6:488
Hiatt, Martha 6:480
Hicks (see Hix), Robt. 6:510; 8:369
Hig(g)don, Dan 7:270, 274, 331, 543, 553; 8:211; 9:656
Higgins, Walter 9:711; Nora 9:742
Higgs, Francis 6:480
Hill, Edw. 7:274, 331, 332, 337, 488, 531, 543; 8:211
  Francis 8:111
  Henry 10:402
  John 9:298
  Jes. 10:336
  Michael 6:327
  Ralph 9:225; 10:222
  Sarah 6:510
  Xto. 9:451
  Walter 7:330
Hilliard, Mary 7:271
  Geo. 7:338
  Tho. 6:613
Hilson, Wm. 7:274
Hilton, Tho. 9:157
Hind, Rich. 335
  Sarah 6:553
  Tho. 6:509
  Wm. 6:227
Hinton, Chris. 6:480
  Edw. 8:75
Hix, Humphry 8:111; 9:394, 397
Hobbins, Wm. 6:510
Hobbs, Abra. 9:391
  John 7:273, 305, 329, 490, 657
  Rich 9:395
Hobby, Tho. 10:337
Hockley, Miles 8:74
Hobson, Jno. 6:286, 510
  Mary 6:286
Hodges, Isabella 9:461
Hodkins, Hannah 9:716
Hofford, _, 7:24

Holder, Anth. 7:657
  Tho. 7:246
Holines, James 8:77
Holland, Rich 10:336
Holliman, Rich. 9:325-519
Hollis, James 7:510
  Eliz. 8:111
Holmes, Matt. 7:330
  Robt. 8:106
  Tho. 6:480
Holsworth, Susan 7:30
  Wm. 8:35
Holt, Roger 8:77
Homes, Geo. 9:714
Honnor, Sarah 9:388
Hoohan, John 9:391
Hooper, Tho. 9:705
Hopkins, Jane 7:274
  John 10:197
Hopp, Tho. 6:447
Hopton, Chas. 9:380
Horbord, Mary 7:124
Horne, Geo. 7:271
  Thos. 9:394
Horner, Roger 7:335
Horons 7:122 Tho.
Horton, Barth 7:336
House, Mary 6:134
How, Matthew 10:198
Howard, Dorothy 8:74
  John 10:340
  Wm. 6:480; 9:461
Howell, John 6:62, 241; 9:85
Howes, Sarah 8:77
Howlett, Geo. 8:76
  Tho. 9:711
Hows, James 7:339
Hudenford, Andrew 6:480
Hudson, _, 9:407
  Rich 10:198
Huet, Robt. 7:246
Hughes, Edw. 7:583
  Eliz. 6:480
  Francis 7:583
  Jane 8:76
  Jno. 6:480
Hughlett, Tho. 10:198
Hunt, Capt. 9:706
  Elinor 9:706
  Hamaway(?) 10:198
  Wm. 8:38; 9:325-519, 390, 391
Hurd, Robt. 7:272
Hurly, Dan. 10:402
Hurling, Wm. 6:480
Hurst, Math. 8:173
Husey, Margt. 9:391
Huson, Kath. 6:480
Hust, Mary 6:480
Hutchison, Edw. 7:78
Hutt, Jiremiah 6:480
Hux, Anth. 8:75
Hyde, Robt. 6:510

Iles, 9:380, Sam
Incas, Ben. 8:71
  Phil 8:71
Inke, W. 6:327
Irby, Edmund 9:420
Ireland, Robt. 9:711
Isham, Hudson 8:78
  Rich. 8:78
Isvill, Sar. 7:29
Ivie, Ruth 10:340
Iybaulds, Robt. 7:30

Jackson, Abra. 8:75
  Geo. 9:706
  John 10:706
  Mihill 6:510
  Ralph 8:244 ; 9:149, 571
  Tho. 9:706

Jacob, Jno. 7:45
Jaines, Annis 9:677
James, Howell 7:339
  Hugh 7:331
  John 6:480
  Mary 9:714
  Sarah 8:55
  Wm. 9:742
Jands, Wm. 7:512
Jamet, Wm. 8:75
Jarvis, Tho. 7:271
Jeffers, Andrew 8:74
Jeffrey, Wm. 8:75
Jells, Hen. 8:211
Jemson, Wm. 9:714
Jenkins, Cath. or Ratherine 6:289
  Jone 9:394
  Wm. 6:189
Jenings, Tho. 7:339
  Eliz 9:656
Jessup, Wm. 9:2
Jettly, Eliz. 6:182
Job, _ (or _ Job) 7:199
Johan, Jane 8:57
Johnson, John 9:298
Johny, Sarah 9:125
Johnson, Capt. 6:90
  Jaquis 8:75
  Jeremy 7:543
  Jacob 9:380
  Jacobus 6:510
  Jno. 7:512; 8:104; 10:402
  Joseph 8:80
  Patrick 7:657
  Simon 9:378
  Wm. 7:30
_ Jone 9:224
Jones, Joanes, Abra. 7:328; 10:401; 8:38, 77
  Abra. Wood J., 7:489
  Anne 6:85; 76
  Fred 9:391
  Gabriel 6: 480
  Hen. 9:378
  Jas. 7:329, 332, 339, 488; 9:460
  Jeremiah 7:512
  John 8:71, 267; 9:391; 10:341
  Kath. 10:10:40
  Margt. 7:252
  Mary 9:677
  Matt. 6:39
  Morris 9:2
  Owen 9:2
  Peter 6:447; 9:224; 10:401
  Rise 6:83
  Rich. 7:328, 654; 9:149, 163, 571; 10:538
  Robert 6:86
  Roger 6:447; 8:104, 369
  Sarah 10:40
  Tho. 6:488; 7:199, 329; 9:391, 714; 10:338
  Wm. 6:510, 529; 7:29, 328, 543, 838, 87, 367, 368; 9:298, 391, 396, 398, 406, 705; 10:197
Joquis, Tho. 8:35
Jorden, Jourdan, Patrick 6:480
  Sam 8:125
Joy, Robt. 8:57
Joyce, Jon 7:330
  Massis 6:510
Joyner, Tho. 9:125
Judseth, John 8:80
Jugles, John 10:042
Jurver, Robt. 6:480

Katherine 7:122
Kay, Jervis 8:57
  Tho. 8:57

Keath, Wm. 7:138
Keeble, Geo. 8:411
Kefhill, Wm. 10:234
Kelleron, Wm. 9:742
Kellett, Robt. 9:525
Kelley, Dan 9:391
  Edw. 9:706
  Math 9:391
  Michael 9:742
  Teague 9:742
  Toby 9:742
Kelsey, Jno. 8:368
Kendall, Eliz. 7:150; 8:244
  Jon 7:339
Kellum, Jon. 7:285
Kempe, John 9:388
Kendall (see above), Eliz. 10:402
Kennedy, Jno. 8:411
  Martha 9:391
Kennold, Edm. 9:742
Kennon, Mary 6:553
Kenselaugh, Arthur 9:706
Kenton, Kath. 9:706
Kerne, David 9:742
Ketty, Law. 9:391
Keys, John 7:575
  Mary 9:461
Kidley, Eliza 407 of Bk. 9
Kieth, Jonas 7:543
Killdolls, Tho. 6:510
Killotty, Sarah 6:292
Kilsony, Wm. 10:198
King, _. 9:338
  Eusebus 7:150
  Hen. 8:76, 368; 9:382, 715
  James 7:535; 9:716
  Sarah 6:510
  Teague 9:742
Kirk, Tho. 7:332
Kish, Eliz 7:303
Kitmore, Sarah 7:331
Knight, Hen. 9:451
  Tho. 9:451
Knott, Wm. 174 of Bk. 8
Kodgeson, Math. 10:198

Ladd, Ed. 6:480; 10:51
Lake, John 7:657
Lambert, Tho. 8:123
Lambud, Wm. 9:397
Lander, Robt. 8:77
Lane, Mary 9:706
  Prissilla 6:480
Langford, Jno. 6:553
Langland, Wm. 6:289, 317
Langly, Rich 8:411
Langman, Langram, Robt. 6:285; 8:173, 411
Lanier, (or Lea), John 7:339
Lar, Mary 10:234
Lashley, Patrick 9:325-519
Laugher, John 9:706
Lawmun, Dan 6:227
Lawrence, Geo. 7:503
  Jno. 6:286; 7:335
Leach, Susan 7:45
Le(a)be(a)ter, _. 6:134
  Francis 7:387; 8:367; 9:298
  Hen. 6:134, 189
  John 8:86, 367; 9:407, 524; 10:299, 320
Lead, John 6:481
Leadens, Hugh 8:25
Leage, Sara 6:286
Leaner (or Lanier, and as accorrection of above Index, not Lea) John 7:339
Lear, _. 7:30
Lee, Ann 6:480
  Hugh 6:480, 519; 7:30, 101, 199, 381, 387, 543; 8:55, 106, 218, 244;

Lee, Hugh Cont. 9:157, 396, 406
  John 6:480; 9:396
  Peter 10:319
  Sam 10:320
  Wm. 6:292
Leech, Tho. 7:657
Leusby(?), Capt. 9:189
Levett, Geo. 7:30
Lewes, Robt. 6:553
  Tho. 10:51
Lewis, Ja. 8:78
  John 6:62; 9:716; 10:403
  Rich 8:77
  Tho. 9:656
Lewison, Wm. 10:336
Lews, Tho. 7:30
Lewton, Tho. 9:382
Liddon, Wm. 9:742
Light, Jno. 7:583
Lilly, Mary 9:706
Linsey, Jno. 9:391
Linsler, Fra. 7:124
Ligon, _. 9:391
Lipwell, Tho. 6:510
Liscomb, Jonas 7:252
Littlegood, Geo. 7:328
Lloyd, Amy 9:391
  Law. 9:391
  Lewis 10:234
  Robt. 9:572
  Tho. 9:711
Lockley, Jno. 8:74
  Mary 8:74
Lolly, Tho. 9:742
Lome, Rebecka 6:510
Long, Eliza 9:157
  Jane 7:331
  Jon. Robt. 7:657
  Waltin 8:77
  Wm. 8:57
Longwell, Rich. 7:150; 8:244; 9:393
Lookman, Rich 9:714
Loope, James 9:742
Louge, James 9:391
Lovet, John 10:234
Lo(w)e, Tho. 7:30, 336, 707; 8:149, 267, 315
  Wm. 8:315; 9:156; 8:71
Lowman, Mary 8:71
Lowry, Lewry, Robt. 6:488; 7:99
Lucas, Margery 6:134
Luce, Eliza 8:71
Lucket, Abra 8:267
Lucy, Capt. 7:554
  Robt. 6:488, 553; 7:303
Lumpton, Jon 7:339
Lyborne, Tho. 7:199; 9:2
Lylly, Tho. 7:253

McCray, John 10:363
McDannell, Hugh 9:742
MacKartes, Cha. 8:71
MacKerry, Cadwalleder 7:510
McLanna 9:742, Jno.
McNaley, Dan. 8:104
Macon, Corn. 9:298
Madard, Ellinor 7:124
Madeboy, Hen. 6:182
Magoone, Jo. 9:395
Mahames, Mary 6:484
Maddox, Joseph 8:244
Maies, Maise, Mays, Mayes, Hen. 10:363, 402
  John 6:134, 481; 7:24, 46
  Matt. 10:401, 402
  Wm. 6:134; 10:198
Mallard, Rich 8:78
Mallory, Susannah 6:480
  Tho. 6:227, 480

Maly, Alex. 7:339
Man, Robt. 8:60
Mandanoll, Mary 9:393
Manering, Hen. 7:45
Manning, Tho. 7:124
Maples, Tho. 8:77, 123
Marble, An. 6:39
March, Rich. 9:388
Marchant, Ja. 6:480
Mark(e)s, Edw. 10:222
  Harritt 10:222
  John 10:222
  Mary 10:222
  Math. 8:77
  Matthihall 10:222
  Sarah 10:222
Marlow, Robt. 10:234
Marsh, Jos. 7:335
  Susan 6:488
Marshall, Dan. 10:336
  Sam 7:192
Martin(e), And. 9:2; 6:529; 9:125; 10:40; 9:157
  Tho. 9:391
  Mary 9:157
Maskew, Isaac 7:244
Mason, Cha. 6:480
Massey, Anne 10:198
  John 10:198
Matham, Jon 7:339
Mathewes, Margaret 6:447
Matons, Danashe (or Daniel) 10:309
  Jas. 9:380
Matter, Robt. 9:380
Maude, John 6:62
Maxfeild, Michael 8:411
Mat(s) & see Maies, Gilbert 7:328
  Hen. 9:711
  John 8:411
  Nich. 9:2
  Wm. 9:718
Mayden, Jon 7:271
Mayson, Tho. 6:488
Meack, Anne 9:742
Meadows, Jno. 8:35
Mealey, Alice 9:742
Meatcham, Joshua 7:122, 407; 8:123
Mercer, Geo. 6:446
Merchant, Rich. 9:714
Merrading, Ja. 9:391
Merritt, Tho. 9:2
Michell, Hen. 10:336
  Peter 10:403
  Tho. 6:510
Midleton, Jon. 7:216
  Robt. 8:55
  Weary 10:234
Miles, Adam 7:216
Millard, Robt. 8:57
Miller, James 8:60
  Roger 8:488
  Tho. 8:369
Millington, Phillis 8:111
Mills, Jas. 7:331
  Sarah 8:74
  Wm. 8:74
  Susan 7:331
Minge, Jas. 9:337, 582
Minter, John 6:289, 317
Mitchell, Edw. 9:388
  Sam 9:742
  Tho. 9:378
Mittaine, Mich 6:273
Moat, Sarah 8:57
Mobell, Alis 6:446
Monaley, Dan 7:535
Moone, Ann 6:510
  Rich 9:391
  Wm. 9:391
Mo(o)r(e), And. 8:71
  Bernard 8:75

Mo(o)r(e), Cont.
  Edw. 8:77
  Eliz. 7:328
  Jane 8:75
  John 7:237, 328; 9:407
  Mary 9:391
  Sarah 8:78
  Theod. 6:480
  Tho. 7:45
  Tuch 10:198
Moorehead, Cha. 9:706
Morgan, David 8:76
  Eliz. 9:391
  Hen. 9:525
  Tho. 6:529; 7:130
  Tim 9:391
Morganhuragon, Hugh 6:529
Morin, Tho. 7:535
Morish, John 9:391
Morley, Anthony 8:173
Moroan, Wm. 8:76
Morris, Adam 7:336; 8:267
  Ellinor 9:742
  John 9:2
  Jas. 10:198
  Margt. 9:742
  Rich 9:715
Mott, Wm. 7:512
Mountford, Jas. 7:192
Moyson, Sam 6:509
Mullins, Margt. 9:742
Mumford, Debora 9:714
  Jas. 7:335, 714
  Robt. 9:714, 715, 718; 10:335, 403, 446
Munge, Jas. 7:330
Murrow, Tho. 7:271

Nasber, Jno. 8:76
Nash, Jeffrey 6:480
Naughty, Jas. 10:40
Nayor, Patrick 9:742
Neale, Hen. 6:510
Nedrent, Chris. 10:363
Neill, Mary 8:75
Nelson, Turler 9:706
Nescrope. Kno. 6:529
Nelson, Geo. 8:78
New 9:125
Nesdin, Rich 6:529
Neting, Wm. 6:286
Nethen, Sam. 9:395
Netherland, Robt. 6:613
Newcomb, Hen. 7:24, 45; 8:411
Newhouse, Tho. 6:182, 227, 289
Newman, Rich 7:535
Newton, Anne 9:2
  Geo. 9:742
  Sarah 8:35
Nicholas, Jno. 6:553, 8:211
  Margt. 9:714
Nicholls, Jas. 8:123
  John 8:135; 10:178, 198, 341
Nindivant, Dan 10:363
Norich, John 9:391
Norman, Rachel 9:461
Norpew, Tho. 9:391
Norris, Roger 7:654
Norton, Elliner 6:553
  Roby 8:78
Notice, Wm. 6:286
Notos, Alex 10:365
Noule, Wm. 7:330
Nowell, Hen. 8:57
  Jane 8:57
  Jon 7:331
  Jno. 8:57
  Wm. 8:57

Occandon, Martha 8:111
Ogle, Wm. 9:395

Ogleby, Cha. 9:716
O Hatcher, Nich. 9:224
O Horn, Alex 9:711
Okeldry, Jas. 6:227
Okey, Robt. 6:85
Olden, Sam. 9:711
Olliver, Eliz. 9:395
  Mary 9:706
  Wm. 9:395
Osborne, Elias 6:142, 406; 7:175
  Jane 7:175
  John 6:142
  Jos. 6:142
  Tho. 8:78
  Wm. 6:142
Oughtye, John 10:336
Overbey, Overley, Nich. 7:45; 8:79; 9:149, 571; 10:234, 401.
Ovy, Tho. 6:510
Owen, Rich. 9:380, 461
  Robt. 10:402
Oxly, Tho. 8:78

Pace, Mr. 6:613
  Rainer alias P. 10:348
  Geo. 9:554
  Rich 6:85; 7:274, 331; 8:211
Packar, Geo. 8:244
Paddon, Jas. 9:439
Page, Ambros 8:75
  Francis 7:546, 564; 8:80
  John 7:446
  Mary 9:461
Pain, Mary 8:411
Pallman, Mich. 6:480
Palmer, Jame 8:71
  Susannah 9:742
Pampin, Tho. 6:189
Panbooke, Rich. 8:74
Parham, Parrum, _. 10:339
  Tho. 8:76; 10:51, 337
Parish, Jos. 10:40
Parker, Dan. 7:253
  Eliza. 10:402
  Ja. 8:75
Parkes, Anne 9:71
Parkham, Wm. 9:392
Parlett, Mary 8:174
Passmore, Geo. 8:368; 9:393; 10:365
  Jon. 7:339
  Jos. 9:394
Pattison, Tho. 7:331
  Martha 9:380
Paul, Griffin 7:543
Pavile, Peter 9:677
Pawlett, Jno. 8:77
Paykervyle, Geo. 9:742
Peacock, Jas. 7:328
Peale, Robt. 10:51
Pecke, Chris. 6:480
  Wm. 7:237
Pedum, Mary 8:60
Peble/Peeble(s), Davis 6:86
  Eliz. 10:342
  Wm. 6:182, 289, 317; 7:339
Peirce, Pierce, Alice 7:543
  Arthur 7:237
  Geo. 9:325-519
Peirson, Tho. 9:714
Pember, Fra. 9:395
Pembic, Alice 9:395
Penis, John 10:335
Pepper, Mary 9:395
Perry, John 9:388
  Jos. 9:189
  Nich. 7:164
Peterson, Ann 6:510
  Jno. 7:30; 10:365

Petingall, Barbara 6:510
Pettypoole, W. 10:338
Peyton, Roger 6:488
Phalan 9:391, Tho.
Phill. 6:480
Phillips, Eliz. 7:285; 9:391;
  Ellinor 9:742
  Jone 8:123
  Mary 7:124, 272
  Rich. 7:45
Phipes, An. 8:71
Pibes, David 7:575
Pirkins, Tho. 8:75
Pitt, Francis 7:657
Platt, Gilbert 6:39
Pledge, Phill. 6:510
Pliner, Mary 9:391
Plowman, Tho. 9:711
Pluckrose, Tho. 9:711
Po-(all), Wm. 9:407
Poisson, Edw. 8:75
Pollard, Sarah 8:111; 9:394
Ponyard, Mary 9:714
Poore, John 9:706
Poove, John 9:706
Popper, _. 8:71
Pott(s), Hen. 7:252
  Tho. 10:151
Porter, Eliz 7:216
  Nich. 7:216
Pourour, John 9:711.
Powell, Wm. 8:57
Poyson, Fra. 6:227
Poythres, Maj. 7:124, 583;
  8:78; 9: 656
  Francis 7:99, 130, 270,
    335, 338, 714, 8:55, 57;
    9:571, 711
  John 7:657; 9:396, 571
Prasock, B. 7:45
Pratt, Gill 7:30
  John 6:248
Prefird, Hen. 6:480
Prescot, Wm. 7:330
Prestor, Robt. 6:613
Price, Edw. 6:286
  Eliz. 8:149
  Hen. 7:328
  Jon 7:328
  Rich. 9:395
  Tho. 9:706
  Wm. 8:111
Prichard, Jno. 8:369; 10:198
  Joshua 10:304
Prince, Rich 7:274
Prior, Peter 8:60
  Winifred 6:447
Prout, Pront, __ 9:2
Purcell, Pursell, Garrett 9:391
  John 9:391
Putman, Eliz. 9:714
  Rich 6:488
Pyder, Tho. 9:706
Pyke, Robt. 9:391

Quin, Tho. 9:391
Quincy, Ellinor 10:40
  Rich. 10:40
  Tho. 10:40
Quinge, John 9:391

Rachell, Ralph 6:406; 7:510
Raclift, Edw. 9:677
Raddish, Tho. 9:742
Ragsdale, Anth. 8:77
Railey, Rich 9:461
Raine, Derby 9:391
Rainer, - alias Face 10:348
Raines, Tho. 10:348
  Wm. 10:77, 349
Ramsey, Tho. 8:77
Randall, Tho. 8:74
Randolph, Hen. 6:246, 247, 248

Randolph, Cont.
  Wm. 7:199; 9:71, 220, 493,
    663
  See Escheator
Rane, Math. 9:380
Rawlins, John 6:273
Ray, John 9:525
Reach, Dorothy 9:711
Read, Abra. 8:35
  Jos. 9:388
  Mary 8:71
Reale, Tho. 9:742
Redding, Timothy 8:218
Redwood, Susanna 10:40
Ree, France 7:512, 542
Reece, John 10:77
Reeding, John 9:711
Reeks, John 7:575
Reese, Roger 7:274
  See Reeves
Reeves, Edm. 7:237
  Robt. 9:706
  Roger 7:543; 8:211
  (R. Roose) & see Reese;
  Tho. 9:325-519
Relfe, Joan 8:75
Rethden, Abrah. 8:123
Revill, Tho. 9:2
Reynolds, Fra. 6:480
  Tho. 6:326
  Wm. 9:461
Rhodes, Jane 7:543
Rice, Rich. 7:328
Richards, Edm. 7:546
  Edw. 6:529
  Pollider 6:488
Richardson, Ellinor 10:40
  Jno. 8:106
  Jos. 10:40
  Robt. 6:510
Richer, Sarah 6:62
Richman, Eliz 9:461
Ridley, Sarah 8:57
Right, Jeremy 6:134
  John 9:525
  Rich 6:529
Risdane, Dennis 9:391
Risese, Roger 6:227
Rives, Robt. 10:197
  Wm. 10:51, 340?
Ro(a)ch, Ellen 7:24
  John 9:706
Roberson, Chris. 10:400
Roberts, Hen. 6:488
  John 8:35; 9:391, 396, 406
  Tho. 9:395
  Wm. 8:123
Robins, Emanuel 8:74
  Tho. 8:106; 10:234
Robinson, Chris. 9:380
  Margaret 8;71
  Nich. 8:55
  Rebecca 6:447
Rockwell, Anne 10:340
  Tho. 7:253
Rogers, John 7:657
  Rich. 8:71
  Wm. 10:199
Roe, Adam 8:74
Rooark, Dennis 9:706
Rookeley, Jane 8:76
  Peter 8:76
Rookes, Roakes, Dorothy 8:57
  John 7:512
  Dan 677
Roomes, Alice 7:244
Roope, Nath. 7:663
Roose, Roger 8:211 & see Reeves
Rope, Math. 8:244
Roper, Jno. 8:75
Rose, Morris 6:247; 7:274
Rouse, Symon 7:335
Row, Phillip 7:275

Row, Cont.
  Scipio 9:991
Rowland, James 7:331
Roye, Robt. 8:211
Royston, Joshua 8:78
Rubye, Jon. 7:335
Rudd 9:391; 398
Rudder, Geo. 8:78
  Tho. 8:57
  Wm. 5:57
Rugsby, Adam 8:75
Russell, Ja. 9:706
  Peter 9:714
Ryland, Jno. 6:488

Sadler, Ed. 7:332
  John 10:40
Salmon, James 9:493
Salter, Rebecca 6:480
Salvage, Wm. 9:676
Sampson, Jane 9:225
  John 8:74
  Mary 9:225
  Step. 9:225
Sanders, Jno. 8:106, 123
Sandes, Lydia 9:391
Sandy, Rebecca 7:45
Sarson, Wm. 7:335
Sattervaile, Wm. 6:39
Savage, Ed. 7:45
  Jno. 8:76
Sawer, Mary 6:488
  John 8:173
Sayer, Tho. 7:332
Sawyer, Lidid 7:199
Saythen, John 9:395
Scafe, Tho. 7:253
Scarbroob, Eliz. 6:488
Scarlett, Tho. 10:198
  See below
Scott, Alex. 9:298
  John 7:446; 8:35 (in text,
    correct "39" to read "35")
    86; 9:325-519, 380, 460,
    493; 10:144
  Tho. 7:575
Scarlett & see above, Anth.
  8:78
  Joan 8:57
Scriven, Onelius 7:138
Seale, Nich. 9:388
Seaman, Peter 6:62
Selby, Hannah 9:714
Selistile, Mary 9:715
Sheone, Honero
Senoir, Tho. 9:523
Sessions, Tho. 10:198
Shapley, Thompson 10:337
Sharpe, Wm. 8:173
Sheffeild, Wm. 7:303
Shaplys, Eliz. 7:164
Shaw, Joh. 7:339
Shelly, John 6:488
Shelson, Fra. 7:338
Shepherd, __ 6:292
Sherney, Jon. 7:339
Shine, Dan. 9:391
Shirly, Jane 9:706
Shomake, Edw. 6:480
Short(e), __ 7:512
  Sam 9:742
  Wm. 6:292; 7:164, 512;
    9:677
Sihes, Sarah 10:234
Simpson, John 7:252, 8:77
Sim(m)ons, Mary 7:657
  Simon 7:657
  Tho. 10:309
Sinckler, Marg. 7:339
Singleton, Wm. 10:197
Slye, Robt. 7:275
Smart, Tho. 9:715
Smelley, Lowis 9:325-519

Smelley, Cont.
  Robt. 9:325-519
  Wm. 9:325-519
Smith, Alice 7:328
  Bryan 7:339
  Eliz. 9:572
  Jas. 7:271, 490
  John 7:10, 216, 466, 536;
    8:244
  Jos. 10:198
  Mary 9:461
  Rich. 6:85; 8:57; 10:335
  Tho. 8:371; 9:395; 10:178
  Sarah 6:62
Smuler, Tho. 9:380
Snart, Alex. 7:575
Snetgrove, Henl. 9:397
Snow, Elsue or Elssie 8:78
Soan, John 8:38
Soper, Elias 9:393
South, Geo. 7:328
Southaway, Wm. 8:111; 9:461
Spackford, Wm. 7:332
Sparks, Rich. 9:125
Spakes, Rich. 6:510
Sparrow, Mr. 6:227
Spell, John 8:111; 9:394
Spencer, Eliz. 10:51
  Mary Hill 9:394
Spenlyn, Rich. 7:30
Spicer, Edw. 7:272
Spike, John 9:380
Springwell, Faith 7:150
Squire, Walter 9:2
Stacy, Tho. 7:216
Stafford, Rich. 6:488
Staley, Rich. 10:340
Standback, N. 9:397
  Wm. 8:111; 9:394
  See Stanbank
Stanbank, etc. Wm., 10:79
Stanley, James 9:706
  Robt. 7:24
Steele, Tho. 8:74
Steevens, Stephens, Edw.,
    10:234
  La. 8:211
  Sarah 7:138
  Tho. 7:138
Stewart, Jon 7:303
  Wm 10:197
Stith, Capt. 9:718
  John 7:244
Stock, Wm. 7:303
Stone, Katherine 7:271
Storidge, Jno. 6:480
Storkes, Anne 9:395
Straham, David 9:395
Strangler, Jane 7:583
Strich,, Jane 9:391
Strickland, Eliz 6:488
Strond, John 10:335
Strong, Straing, Tho. 9:711
  Adus 9:711
Stroud, Tho, 7:30
Stuard, Cha. 6:509
  Sarah 9:391
Sturden, Dan. 9:87
Sturdevant, John 6:327, 480;
    8:60
Sturges, Jno. 9:395
Surgill, Eliz. 9:715
Sutton, Alex 10:77
Swarter, (?), Martha 10:342
Swellame, Sarah 6:510
Swift, Tho. 8:71
Swinboarne, Bartho. 7:331
Sydenham, Eliz. 9:461
Symons, Hen. 7:332
  Jno. 9:391
  Oliver 7:339

T (as in Ms.), Robt. 8:60
Tally, Hen. 8:86; 9:224
  John 10:340
  Rich 10:337
Tance, Tho. 6:510
Tannard, Cha. 10:197
Tanner, Jas. 7:216
  Tho. 7:488
Tapley, Adam 8:57, 78; 9:711
Tarkin, Anth. 8:75
Tatum, Nath. 6:241; 9:85;
    10:309, 322, 341
  Nich. 6:203
  Sam 7:536; 8:86; 9:380;
    10:316, 341
Tayloe, Wm. 8:111
Taylor, Edm. 7:246
  Elianor 9:461; 10:402
  Jos. 10:40
  Rich. 6:488
  Rey 9:656
  Tho. 6:553
  Valen 7:303
  Wm. 6:510
Teage, 6:480
Tecke, And. 6:553
Tedder, Mary 8:111
Tegamy, Elias 7:30
Tempell, Wm. 8:86
Temple, Sam. 9:711
  Wm. 9:524; 10:299
Terrill, Robt. 6:39
Terry, Dr. 7:575
  John 7:512, 542
  Tho. 9:380
Testervill, Festervill, Lucy
    8:106
Thacker, E. E. 9:742
Theary, James 9:706
Thomas, Ann 6:510
  John 7:138; 3:111
  Mary 7:328
  Wm. 7:272
Thornbury, Rich 7:335
Thornton, James 8:75
Throer, John 6:447
Throgmorton, Jno. 8:77
Thrower, Tho. 9:393
Thurwell, Sam. 9:714
Thweate, Jas. 6:286, 446,
    447, 486; 7:150, 708;
    8:368; 9:393
Tillett, John 9:380
Ti(l)lman, Geo. 10:52
  Roger 7:338, 707; 8:71, 74,
    76
Tivey, Tho. 9:225 (125?)
Toats, Eliz. 8:71
Tomlinson, Tho. 6:289, 317
Tool, Ann 10:40
Thompson, Eliz. 9:677
  Jane 9:677
  John 6:480
  Margt. 9:677
  Mary 9:677
  Peter 7:328
  Robt. 9:407
  Wm. 9:677
Tood, Ben. 6:553
Toolye, Tho. 7:336
Tophler, Jno. 8:71
Tovey, Jno. 6:480
  Jos. 6:480
Townesend, Hannah 6:529
Towsing, Anne 6:488
Trehoane, Jno. 6:182
Trainer, Tho. 6:529
Trape, Tho. 9:391
Trea, Law. 9:742
Treake, Peter 8:75
Trefry, Joane 7:512
Trenmett, Jno. 6:510

Tromsin(?), Wm. 10:222
Try, Peregrine 7:306
Trydon, Mart 7:45
Tucher & see Tucker, John
    10:338
  Jos. 10:339
Tucker & see Tucher, Fra.
    10:339, 402
  John 7:29, 253; 9:380
  Jos. 10:402
  Robt. 7:29, 535; 10:340
  Wm. 10:403, 446
Tunstall, etc. Edw. 6:134
  Rich. 8:55; 6:481
Turberfeild, Rich. 8:267
Turges, Simon 10:40
Turner, Ann 7:331
  Barth. 8:35
  Jno. 8:76
  Margt. 7:216
Turpin, Wm. 7:124
Tuthill, James 7:663
Tuttle, Wm. 9:451
Tutton, Hen. 7:339
Tye, Rich. 6:86

Underwood, Jno. 8:174
Unebill, Robt. 61484
Unit, John 9:656
Vaudin or Vandin, Clare
    8:60
  Paul 8:60
Vaughan, Ellin:r 8:111
  Hester 8:111
  Jas. 8:35
  Mary 8:35
  Wm. 7:30, 654; 9:156
Vernon, Hen. 7:274
Vickary, Edm. 7:545
Voss, Tho. 8:35
Veyer, Jane 10:446,
  John 10:446

WaMire, Abra 9:677
Walke, James 9:714
Walker, __ 10:316
  John 9:380, 461, 706
  Wm. 6:488
Wall, He. 8:76, 77; 9:149,
    163
Wallace, Mr. 7:303, 510
  Eliz. 8:80; 9:461
  Jas. 6:248, 553; 7:122,
    338; 8:55, 80; 9:380
  John 8:55, 368
  Mary 8:80; 9:388
  Rich. 8:411
Wallis, Hen. 9:571
Wallman, Tho. 8:211
Wallow, Tho. 6:480
Walls, Geo. 9:388
Wampoole, John 7:138; 8:174
Wapple, John 9:676
Ward, Jas. 7:657
  John 6:227
  Robt. 6:509
  Sam 8:71
Wardon, Jon 7:330
Warradine, etc., Mr. 7:192,
    270; _, 10:125
  Jas. 6:285; 7:338; 8:173,
    411; 9:438
Warren, Rich. 6:510; 7:306
  Sam 6:85
  Wm. 9:2
Washbrooke, Ja. 6:509
Washington, Arthur 9:325-519
  John 9:325-519
  Rich. 7:464; 9:325-519
Waters, Giles 8:111
Watson, Ja. 8:75
  Rich. 6:510
Watts, Jer. 8:35

Wayder, Wm. 7:339
Weaner, Jon 7:339
Webber, Rich. 7:312 (512?)
Webster, Ja. 8:?4
  Wm. 8:77
Welch, etc. John 8:77, 123;
  9:391
  Morgan 7:335
Wells, Adam 8:77
  Honor 9:742
  Robt. 8:70
  Tho. 8:77
Welly, Ann 8:60
West, Geo. 7:328
  Hen. 7:216
  John 6:248, 480; 8:60
  Mary 7:216, 512
  Rich 7:328
  Robt. 6:285; 8:411
  Wm. 8:60; 9:388; 10:336(?)
Westbrooks, Wm. 10:042
Weyes, Robt. 9:571
Weysh, Hen. 7:339
Whale, Tho. 9:407
Whaley, Robt. 8:57
Wharton, Jno. 8:77
  Sarah 8:76
Wheelehouse, Rich. 8:55; 9:2
Wheeler, Eliz. 7:510
  Fra. 9:706
  Mary 9:706
  Rich 8:267
  Tho. 6:248
Wheelan, Edw. 9:391
Whitby, Jane 8:77
White, Dorothy 8:173
  Eliza 8:106
  Hen. 7:164
  Alice 9:706
  Joan 9:2
  Jon 7:336; 8:55
  Robt. 8:78
  Sarah 8:77
  Tho. 7:332
  Tim 8:75
Whiteker, Avis 9:380
Whithall, John 9:451
Whiting, Jno. 8:78
  Mary 7:271
Whitmore, Nich. 7:124; 8:78
Whittington, __ 6:62, 481
  Fra. 6:484
  Wm. 7:633
Whood, Tho. 10:336
Wiggins, Hen. 9:380
Wigmore, Ruth 8:77
Wilbison, Wm. 7:285
Wilcox, An. 7:138
Wilkins, John 9:706
  Wm. 6:85; 7:272, 305;
    8:370
Wilkinson, John 7:512
  Rich. 9:572
  Tho. 8:71
  Wm. 9:714
Williams, Cha. 9:451; 10:51,
  338
  David 10:336
  Eliz. 6:286
  Geo. 9:391
  Jas. 9:451
  John 6:286; 7:124, 331,
    553, 554; 8:55; 9:451,
    656
  Paul 7:332
  Rachel 6:286
  Rich 9:378
  Sarah 7:546
  Tho. 6:480; 7:543
  Wm. 6:286, 509; 9:325-519,
    519
William, King of Eng. 9:221
Williamson, Geo. 9:325-519

Williamson, Cont.
  John 7:543; 8:211; 9:461
  Leonard 10:234
  Rich. 7:237; 9:125
Willis, Eliz. 8:35
  Jane 7:543
Willoughby, Edw. 8:57
  Jno. 8:78
Wills, Solomon 9:391
Wilmott, Susanna 7:274
Wilskins, Robt. 10:198
Wilson, Joan 8:75
  Jno. 6:613
  Matt. 7:216
  Robt. 8:77
  Tho. 10:234
  Wm. 7:512; 10:402
Windham, Cha. 9:714
Winfeild, Anne 9:393
Wingame, Jon 7:150
Wishett, Anth. 7:45
Witches, Hen. 7:381
Withers, John 9:718
With (__, blank 2 letters)nke,
  Rich. 10:341
Witt, Jon 7:199; 9:2
Woaver, Wm. 8:75
Wolly, Tho. 8:60
Wooan, Wm. 9:380
Wood(s), Col. 8:76, 77
  Maj. Gen. 7:276
  Abra 7:45, 328
  Aron 8:77
  Eliz 6:484; 9:461
  Jane 8:77
  Jno. 6:553
  Mary 8:411
  Robt. 8:77
  Tho. 6:510; 7:335
  Wm. 7:335
Woodbridge, Susanna 10:40
Woodby, Robt. 7:216
Woodcock, Elinor 6:446
Woodley, John 7:335
Woodliffe, etc. Edw. 10:320
  Eliz. 9:388
  John 7:714; 9:718
Woodnell, John 7:575
Woodward, __ 9:87
  Chris. 7:24; 8:411
  Joan 9:714
  Sam 6:34, 481, 509; 7:24, 45
Wool, Eliz 10:40
Wootton, Hen. 8:75
Wopley, Mary 8:60
Worley, Mary 8:411
Worthington, Tho. 7:46
Wrack, Jarvis 8:57
Wray, Andrew 8:74
Wright, __ 9:157
  Giles 6:289, 317
  John 7:388, 339; 9:157
  Rich. 6:62, 509
  Sam 9:2
  Wm. 8:77
Wyatt, Capt. 7:512
  Anth. 6:247, 509
  Nich. 7:510, 531
  Robt. 6:488
Wyke, Peter 7:339
Wynn, Frances 10:199
  Godfrey 6:48
  Jno. 7:543, 583
  Peter 10:309
  Robt. 10:341
  Tho. 7:583; 8:55; 9:406;
    705

Yapp, Jno. 6:227
Yeates, Matthew 9:663
  Phil. 6:553
  Tho. 8:75
Yeo, John 7:272

Yeoman(s), Mary 7:285
  Tho. 9:716
York, Tho. 9:714
Young, Barbara 7:150
  Edw. 6:447

Blacks

Able 8:371
Abra. 8:111
Ben 7:271
Buck 8:371
Diana 8:77
Dick 8:76
    8:86
    8:149
    9:85
Doe 8:371
Fran 8:86
Gay 8:244
Gerald 8:371
Grace 8:75
Guy 8:104
    9:85
Harry 8:86
Jack 8:86
    9:85
    9:157
Jane 9:85
Jenny 8:111
Judy 8:86
Mary 6:54
Mareton 8:371
Mingo 8:371
Mungo 6:480
Nan 9:85
Nanse 8:149
Ned 8:76
Nell 8:76
    9:2
Nick 8:104
Nora 9:85
Pelighey 8:149
Pompey 8:24
Robin 8:77
Rosse 8:86
Ruth 8:76
Sam 8:104
Sambo 8:76
    8:86
    8:104
Santall 8:371
Sarah 8:371
Simon 9:24
Sus 8:371
Susanna 8:376
Tango 7:150
Timoth 7:150
Thos. 6:613
Tom 8:76
    8:149
Tony 8:104
    8:106
Walter 9:85
Wassa 8:104

Three not named 7:24
Three not named 5:12
Twenty not named 9:2
Three not named 9:378

There are also three whites not named.

PLACE INDEX

Banks, Va. S. side, Mussell Shell Bank 6:406
Baylys (Land called) 8:411
Blackwater, the 6:447, 480, 486, 488, 510, 553; 7:29, 30, 99, 101, 122, 351, 464, 469, 503, 535, 543, 633, 654, 709; 8:55, 57, 104, 127, 174, 175, 368; 9:221, 325-519, 388, 460, 571, 582, 711; 10:198
Bays, Swans Bay 6:404
Bottoms, Mr. Byrd's 6:142
 Dry B. 7:714, 718
 Hancock's, etc. 6:142, 406
 Reedy B. 6:86
Branches, Alder Br. 7:381
 Ante Church see Colechurch
 Ashen 8:55, 244; 10:338
 Bland 8:55
 Boggy 6:529
 Cabbin 10:51
 Cattle, etc. 6:62, 553; 7:303; 8:71
 Cherry 7:330, 332
 C. Orchard Br. 9:393
 Solechurch, etc. 9:339
 Cotchurch 9:393
 Cow 8:76
 Cross 9:714
 Doby's John 9:338
 Edloes 9:397, 398
 Ellington's 10:338, 339
 Flinities 10:51
 Glandy 10:337
 Great, see text 7:536, 707; 8:75, 76; 10:77, 178, 304, 320, 337, 339
 Hog Pen 8:55, 10:51
 Hollow Bush 7:270
 Horne 7:335
 Horse Pen 10:336, 446
 House Path Br. 7:101
 Indian, etc. 10:336, 337
 Jones Hole Br. 9:157, 337
 Kibbey 10:144
 Little 9:338
 L. Hell or Stricks (or Hicks) 10:51
 Long Point Br. 7:274
 Lows 10:335
 Lower Kings Field 7:274, 543; 8:211
 Upper F. 7:274, 543; 8:211
 Main;291
 Meadow Br. 9:71, 221
 Myery 9:396
 Parting 9:337
 Poplar 9:291
 Northern 7:244, 252
 Quagmire 9:676
 Reedy 7:29, 124, 216, 554; 8:57, 106; 9:220, 224, 493, 706, 711
 R. Bottom Br. 7:657; L0:315, 403
 Rohowick, etc. 7:328; 8:38; 9:149, 163
 Solmonds Meadow Br. 9:396
 Southern 7:335; 9:225
 Middle S. Br. 7:270
 Spring 9:741
 Squabling 10:402 & see text
 Stony, 10:403
 Tanners 7:331
 Trading 9:406
 Unities 10:51
 Western 7:216; see 3 lines below
Bridge, Dobys 10:322

Bridges, Old Town B. 6:86
Branches, Tumio Readings 9:337
Bycars 7:338
Canatorah, place called 9:395
Charles City, the City 6:62
Church Landing 10:40
 C. Glebe 10:40
College Land 9:339, 390
Creeks, Appawhipoats 6:292
 Balles 7:583
 Ban (all of word) 6:62
 Barlethorpe, etc. 9:337, 338, 395, 396
 Baylyes, etc. 6:62, 203, 285, 286, 484, 486; 7:46; 8:173, 411; 9:439; 10:199
 Beaverdam 9:388
 Bickers, Etc. 7:531; 9:718 Greek
 Bridge Cr. 7:272; 8:370
 Buckskin 10:403
 Caresons, Ca(w)sons 6:203, 241, 62
 Cattaile 6:481
 Chetehegraph, cr Sw. 9:741, etc.
 Chippoaks, etc. 10:40
 C. Upper 6:273, 404; 7:138, 164, 513, 542, 575; 8:174; 9:523, 676, 677
 Cross 10:125
 Ellis 9:291
 Flewerdieu & F. Hun. 6:85, 613; 7:657
 Grabally 6:62
 Great, of Nottoway Riv. 10:338
 Hackery 10:40
 Indian Town Cr. 7:45
 Island 9:391
 Lappen(e), 10:335, 336, 446
 Leadbeter's 10:234
 Little, Surry Co. (?) 10:349
 Mawhipponock 10:339, 401, 402
 Merchants Cr. etc. 6:90
 Moccosoneck, etc. 9:714; 10:52, 337, 338, 339, 403
 Monofineck 10:335
 Monkes(e) 9:392, 420
 Monous Neck Cr. 9:382
 Nannesons 10:336, 337, 338, 339, 340
 Neards, 6:529
 Persimon 8:315
 Powell's 7:657; 10:40
 Stony 9:714; 10:221, 367, 402, 446
 Swift 7:273
 Wallis 10:401
 Wards 6:142, 406; 7:332, 512
Deep Bottom, Land called 9:396
Field, Conatora Old F. 9:396
 Indian 6:529; 9:378; 10:336
Fords, Wombepoak, 10:337
Fort, F. Lands 7:328
Guts, Simson's 10:199
High Peake, Land called 8:411; 9:438-9
Hole, Cone H. 9:398
 James 10:77
 Jones 9:338, 395, 396, 398, 406, 705; 10:77, 336
Islands, Great I. 9:741
Lands, Indian Town L. 7:328
Level, Faleroot 9:711
 Poplar, etc. 10:125

Jones, etc. 10:125
Marsh, Tappahannock 10:40
Martin Brandon, Land called 10:40
Meadows, Baley's 8:218
 Cattayle 10:52
 George's 10:198, 341; 9:582
 Great, the 7:199, 8:123
 Long 9:711
 Myry, etc. 7:407; 8:123
 Oatcoes 9:394
 Small 8:371
 Warwick 9:189; 10:316
 White 7:332
Merchants, etc. 6:488; 10:40, 125
Necks, Hangmans 7:272; 8:370
Moncusoneck 8:71, 74, 76, 244
Moneasoneck 8:315
Monkey's 8:267; 9:392
Mounteys 7:336
New Rutland 9:337, 338
Nuntora 9:380
Old Town 7:331
Otterdams 7:237, 246, 339; 8:38, 86; 9:71, 125, 221
Paths, Baylys 7:46
 Blackwater 7:554
 Blands 6:85; 7:272, 285; 8:370
 Cunatora 9:400
 Horick 9:225
 Jordans 7:29
 Mill 7:272, 332, 488; 8:370
 Nannisonas, etc. 10:337, 401
 Nottoway 7:99, 381; 8:71; 9:396, 572
 Nuskarora, or Road 9:395
 Oosomonock 10:402
 Onominche 10:309, 337
 River 10:336, 337, 339
 Tonotura 7:381
 Trading, Lower T. P. 9:398
 Western T. P. 9:571
Place, Tohinnk fyling P. 9:378
Points, Long 7:543
 P. of Rocks 8:25
Ponds, Beaver 7:707
 Great B. 8:38
Piney 10:403, Pond
Round 7:124; 8:369; 9:149, Pond.
R. Point P. 7:246
Powhiponack 8:75
Rivers, Appamattocks, etc. 6:39, 134, 189, 203, 241, 286, 327, 446, 447, 480, 481, 484, 486, 509, 510; 7:24, 30, 45, 46, 199, 328, 336, 387, 489; 7:535, 707, 708; 8:25, 38, 75, 80, 86, 104, 267, 315, 411; 9:163, 224; 10:337, 340
Hepouatuck 7:216
James 6:62, 85, 86, 182, 203, 227, 289, 317, 488, 529, 553; 7:30, 99, 124, 150, 164, 192, 237, 244, 246, 252, 270, 274, 273, 285, 303, 305, 329, 331, 332, 335, 337, 469, 488, 490, 531, 543, 553, 554, 583, 657, 714; 8:78, 123

Rivers, James - Cont.
  211; 9:125, 220, 325-519,
    420, 524, 571, 656; 10:40,
    178
  Nottoway, etc. 9:157, 7093377,
    378, 390, 391, 392, 394,
    395, 396, 397, 398, 406,
    706, 714; 740, 741, 742;
    10:197, 304, 315, 338,
    340, 365, 40, 403
  Winding 7:24
Roads, Barrow's 9:677
  Great 7:338
  Kings 7:24, 192
  Nuskarora see Paths
  Puidia(?) 10:304
  Warwick Main R. 9:582
Rohdwick 8:76, 77; 9:571
Row_am 7:543, 8:106
Runs, Cattaile & Poll 7:274
  Codper(?) 10:304
  Dry Bottom 7:192, 335
  Gravely 9:451
  Hatchers 8:74, 111, 149;
    10:198
  Hutchens 10:198
  Hofford 7:24
  Mohouaneck 7:707
  Pole, etc. 7:274, 330, 332
  Ponns Main R. 7:273; 10:241
  Reedy 9:224
  Southern 6:85, 529; 7:216
    8:75; 10:222
  Wards 8:77
  Western 9:676, 677
  W. Wad. 9:149
Counties: Nans, Upper Par.
    7:503 ?
  I. of W., 8:174
  Surry 6:292; 9:676; 10:349
Slashes, Cold 7:164
  Long 6:481
  Piny 7:339
  Round Pond's 9:571
  Woolfes 7:192
Snow Hill 9:382
Spring, Blackwater 9:572
Swamps, Acomorock 9:460
  Bear 10:337
  Beaver, Dam Sw. 9:392, 393
  Blackwater 9:493, 519, 571;
    10:51, 342
  Burchens, etc. 6:182, 227,
    289, 317; 7:339
  Butterwood's 10:304, 309,
    338-9,
  Cabbin Stick 9:394
  Correhuesoe 9:397
  Great 6:134, 292, 481;
    7:335, 8:55
  Hatchers Main Sw. 9:156
  Harry 9:741
  Herdam 8:371
  Holloway 9:519
  Indian 9:392, 393, 396, 397
  Jones Hole Sw. 9:393, 493;
    10:198, 309, 336, 348
  Joseph 9:337, 338, 339,
    378, 380; 10:304, 309, 322,
    341
  Main 7:99, 122, 199, 274;
    8:367, 368
  Mocconseneck Main Sw. 8:149;
    9:156
  Otterdam, etc. 8:371; 10:178
  Pigion, etc. 9:71, 220, 221
  Poiney 6:189
  Rowanty 9:714
  Second 8:55, 60, 244, 369;
    10:338, 363
  Severed(?) 10:309
  Southern 7:328
  Warwick 7:381; 8:35, 367;

Warwick, Cont. 9:189, 298,
  10:144, 299, 319, 320
Waughnick 7:199
White Oake 9:420; 10:400,
  402
Worwick 9:380, 407, 524,
  525
Warrishes 9:493
Wildcat fall down 8:244
Werrosknock 7:387, 536

SUBJECTS

Va., Auditor 9:706
  see Wm. Byrd.
Books: Nugent, Cavaliers 8:125
College, Wm. & Mary 9:221
Parishes, Bristol 7:24, 45,
    46, 101, 199, 216, 328,
    336, 387, 489, 535, 536,
    543, 633, 654, 707, 708,
    709; 8:25, 35, 60, 74,
    75, 76, 77, 80, 104, 106,
    111, 148, 218, 244, 267,
    315, 367, 368, 369, 411,
    9:87, 148, 157, 163, 224,
    291, 298, 382, 407, 451,
    571;
  B. Court 6:509
  Jordans 7:124, 150, 335,
    469, 531, 583; 8:78, 244
  Martin Brandon 6:90
  (a Patent to) 326; 7:164,
    510; 8:77; 9:225
  Westover 7:122, 192, 244,
    252, 270, 274, 285, 303,
    331, 337, 339, 488, 543,
    553, 554, 657, 714;
    8:211, 370; 9:656
  Weyanoke 7:237, 246, 273,
    305, 329, 332, 490, 657;
    9:71, 125, 220

Positions; Auditor 9:706;
  See Byrd Escheator & Dep. E.
  See Heh, Randolph, Hen, Hart-
    well, John Page, Fr. Page, Wm.
    Randolph.
Pr. Geo. Co. line 10:316, 342,
  446
S. side trading and other relations
  with Great Britain, London,
  see: John Sadler, the Rev.
  Joseph Richardson, Tho.
    Quiney, Simon Sturges,
    Richard Quinrey,
    Scotchman, David a S. 6:227

www.ingramcontent.com/pod-product-compliance
Lightning Source LLC
Chambersburg PA
CBHW031428290426
44110CB00011B/577